Making Sense of
English in
Religion

English in Use Series

General Editor: David Crystal

Making Sense of
English in
Religion

Laurence Twaddle

EDINBURGH   NEW YORK

Published 1992 by W & R Chambers Ltd
43–45 Annandale Street, Edinburgh EH7 4AZ

© Laurence Twaddle 1992

A catalogue record for this book is available from the
British Library

ISBN 0-550-18045-1

Typeset by Æsthetex Ltd, Edinburgh
Printed in England by Clays Ltd, St Ives plc

Contents

Preface

The language of intelligent people is sprinkled, often unwittingly, with the jargon of religious language. Indeed, the whole of our culture is immersed in ideas and technical terms that have their roots in the religious thought of the Judaeo-Christian experience, which we have absorbed into our thinking and literature more perhaps than we are aware.

People are described as being an 'angel' or a little 'devil'. They are accused jokingly of telling 'apocryphal' stories, of being a bit of a 'zealot', or of being rather 'dogmatic'. They preface their claims with the assurance that this is 'gospel' truth, while describing others as 'cult' figures or pop 'icons'.

Without much awareness of the background, men and women page 'Oracle®' on their TV, describe visiting granny at the weekend as a bit of a 'penance', consider people who didn't like the movie *Apocalypse Now* to be real 'Philistines', reckon the time spent in the dentist's waiting-room to be sheer 'purgatory' or even absolute 'hell'. Wondering if the car salesman is really 'kosher', they grow anxious at the thought of making financial 'sacrifices', recall how their job interview was like the Spanish 'Inquisition', and long for a cool drink of whatever on the beach of their island 'Paradise'. Why, that would be just sheer 'heaven'. They consider their next-door 'neighbour' to be a 'relic' from an earlier age, whose 'revelations', sometimes verging on 'blasphemy', about life in their streets are not 'infallible' in spite of his 'cherubic' smile.

And all this before we explore the impact of other world religions on the language we use so easily, often without too much awareness of their full religious significance.

English Words In Religion is a book that aims to fill in the background to the religious language we find in regular use – ideas and thought-forms that people are in the habit of introducing into their conversation.

Because the Judaeo-Christian influence has been so deep and widespread within our Western society, clarifications are weighted in that direction; investigation is, however, liberally spiced with half-familiar concepts from other world faiths and religious philosophies.

Laurence Twaddle

Pronunciation Guide

Vowels

iː	need	/niːd/
ɪ	pit	/pɪt/
i	very	/ˈvɛri/
ɛ	pet	/pɛt/
æ	pat	/pæt/
ʌ	other	/ˈʌðəʳ/
ʊ	book	/bʊk/
uː	too	/tuː/
u	influence	/ˈɪnfluəns/
ɒ	cough	/kɒf/
ɔː	ought	/ɔːt/
ɜː	work	/wɜːk/
ə	another	/ənˈʌðəʳ/
ɑː	part	/pɑːt/

Glides

eɪ	plate	/pleɪt/
aɪ	sigh	/saɪ/
ɔɪ	ploy	/plɔɪ/
oʊ	go	/goʊ/
aʊ	now	/naʊ/
ɪə	hear	/hɪəʳ/
ɛə	fair	/fɛəʳ/
ʊə	poor	/pʊəʳ/

Consonants

p	pit	/pɪt/
b	bit	/bɪt/
t	ten	/tɛn/
d	den	/dɛn/
k	cap	/kæp/
g	gap	/gæp/
ʃ	shin	/ʃɪn/
ʒ	pleasure	/ˈplɛʒəʳ/
ʧ	chin	/ʧɪn/
ʤ	budge	/bʌʤ/
h	hit	/hɪt/
f	fit	/fɪt/
v	very	/ˈvɛri/
θ	thin	/θɪn/
ð	then	/ðɛn/
s	sin	/sɪn/
z	zones	/zoʊnz/
m	meat	/miːt/
n	knit	/nɪt/
ŋ	sing	/sɪŋ/
l	line	/laɪn/
r	rid	/rɪd/
j	yet	/jɛt/
w	quick	/kwɪk/

ʳ indicates an 'r' pronounced only before a following vowel
ˈ precedes the syllable with primary stress

Guide to Readers

Bold type, eg **abbot** at **abbey**, **Golgotha** at **Calvary** and **Vedantar** at **Veda**, is used to draw the reader's attention to related words that are not themselves entries.

A

abbey

A religious community under the leadership of an *abbot* or *abbess*, housed in a building or group of buildings known as an *abbey*. In the Middle Ages the great abbeys were centres of wealth and learning, and were looked on with envy by the aristocracy, covetous of their treasures. (See also **monasticism**.)

absolution

A declaration of forgiveness of sins, pronounced by a priest or minister. Within the liturgy of some major branches of the Christian Church, the form of worship includes the pronouncing of such forgiveness by a priest or minister in the name of the Saviour Jesus, following a public or private act of confession. It is stressed that this is seen only as an outward statement of a reality brought about by Jesus. The priest or minister is merely the herald of that forgiveness achieved by Jesus, and is in no way its author. (See also **penance**; **reconciliation**.)

Advent

The coming of the one for whom the world has been waiting (the Deliverer, Saviour, or Messiah), whose arrival spells the end of the old age and the inauguration of the Kingdom of God. It is a season of expectation, and preparation is a key factor in the Advent mood and experience. John the Baptist, the herald of the Advent of Christ, calls the people to a frame of mind which will enable them to be receptive to the King who comes, and to be ready for the Kingdom he brings. Traditionally, in the Christian liturgical calendar, Advent is celebrated during the four weeks prior to Christmas itself. (See also **Messiah**.)

Adventists

An element in Christianity where the theology is dominated by the idea of an imminent return of Jesus to this earth. The term covers a wide range of groups and individuals emerging through-out the story of the Church, offering a variety of proposed dates for this re-appearance. The most enduring group, and the one which has edged its way towards a degree of acceptability within mainstream Christianity, is the Seventh Day Adventist Church, founded in the USA by William Millar, who predicted a date of 1843 for a literal Second Coming. The conviction of this sect is that the Second Coming has not happened because, in particular, the practice of respecting the old Jewish Sabbath falling on the seventh day is being flouted. It will only be when the Sabbath is acknowledged and duly marked that the Second Coming will take place. (See also **millenarianism**.)

agnosticism

The view that God cannot really be known as such, or at least, that it is not possible to be convinced either way by the evidence presently available. The origin of the term lies in the Book of Acts, where Paul is described in debate in Athens over a statue to 'an unknown God'; the word was introduced into English by T H Huxley in 1869. Agnosticism is often expressed as an indication of an open mind – but it could equally be interpreted as the last refuge of a lazy mind, unwilling to pursue the arguments to one end or the other. (See also **atheism**; **theism**.)

Allah

The Islamic name for God. Rooted in the cultures of Arabia, Allah had reigned supreme among deities, but it was the mission of Mohammed to herald Allah as the one true God – the creator and sustainer of all things and the judge of all humanity. Allah makes his will known in the Holy Book of the Koran, revealed gradually to his servant and prophet Mohammed. (See also **Islam**.)

altar

A table or platform where sacrifice is carried out. Offerings may be burnt to please God or a god or in obedience to his instructions. In many religions it is a focal point, the place where the central act of worship takes place. For example, in modern Roman Catholic churches, the altar is where the Mass is celebrated and the holy Sacrament made available to the people. (See also **sacrifice**.)

Anabaptists

One of the radical religious groups which emerged from the
Reformation determined to out-reform the Reformers. Their
particular enthusiasms were the restriction of baptism to believers
and their refusal to accept the validity of infant baptism. Their
radicalism reached out to include adherence to the literal word
of scripture, strict church discipline, and the clear separation of
church and state – a doctrine which brought them severe persecution. They were the forerunners of the Baptists, who share many
of the convictions and emphases of these early radicals. (See also
Baptists.)

angel

A messenger from God, called to serve him, and to appear at
crucial moments in human history with news or instructions of
particular significance. These heavenly beings have no honour
or status in themselves, and are not to be worshipped in any
way. They are simply there to do a job – deliver a message. Some
angels are more famous than others, Gabriel and Michael being
given particular status. The dark side of angels is discerned in the
speculation that Satan himself is a fallen angel, rebelling against
God, and joined in his rebellion by other 'fallen angels'. (See also
cherub; **Gabriel**; **Michael**; **Satan**.)

Anglican Communion

A worldwide fellowship of 26 independent provincial or national
churches, several extra-provincial dioceses, and other churches
sharing close ecclesiastical and doctrinal relationships with the
Church of England. The missionary zeal of the Church in the
19th century led to the emergence of many churches throughout
the old British Empire, and the British Commonwealth is now
the main home of the Anglican Communion. Other countries,
however, found inclusion, notably the Episcopal Church of the
USA (which was fostered by the Scottish Episcopal Church),
while other non-Commonwealth countries such as Japan, China
and Brazil also contain churches which are part of the Anglican
Communion. Although there is no formal body with ultimate
authority, the long historical link with England has led, every
ten years, to the Archbishop of Canterbury inviting bishops from

within this worldwide communion to the Lambeth Conference to consider matters of common interest and concern. The independence of member churches, however, is not in any way challenged by what is largely a consultation process. (See also **Church of England**.)

Anglo-Catholic

A movement within the Anglican Church in the 19th century, aiming to rediscover the place of the sacraments and creeds in Christian faith, and in concert with the wider Catholic Church (especially the Roman Catholic Church) to express that essential unity lost at the Reformation. High Church liturgy, a re-emphasis upon the role of Mary, and a strong desire to rediscover the lost fellowship of the once truly Catholic Church are the recognizable ingredients of the Anglo-Catholic experience. (See also **Catholic**; **Church of England**; **Oxford Movement**; **Roman Catholicism**.)

animism

In primitive religions, the conviction that all living things are animated by spirits, different from humans only in their degree of power. It is thought that this basic spiritual viewpoint lies at the beginning of the search for religious meaning wherever that quest is encountered. Animism can still be found practised by many millions in cultures which have remained largely untouched by modern intrusions. The belief that the whole universe is the area of activity for a realm of spirits is deep and powerful among these peoples, who see spirits at work in nature, fire, wind and rivers, the spirits of the dead still a reality to be dealt with, and special spirits inhabiting sacred places and being free and creative forces in the world. Often fear is the dominant emotion inspired by this unknown and disturbing spiritual realm, and the role of magic and superstition is significant.

Annunciation

The event recorded in the Gospel of Luke when the Angel Gabriel tells Mary that she will give birth to Jesus, and declares her particular role and greatness. It is also the occasion on which the faith and humility of Mary are represented, and the occasion on which she expresses her joy and surprise that God has chosen a humble girl to bring forth his Saviour, a merciful act which confounds the proud and the great. (See also **Virgin Birth**.)

4

anointing

An act in which, by the symbolic pouring of oil on the head, individuals are recognized to be set apart for a particular divine task or duty. Olive oil, held to have particular qualities of healing and spiritual significance, was used in the act. Anointing was the sign of a special favour and a summons to a particular task. Indeed, the name *Christ* means 'the anointed one', set apart to deliver Israel and bring in the Kingdom of God. In New Testament thought, the Holy Spirit became the anointing agent, not the visible sign of oil. Jesus first, and then the whole Church, came to be anointed with the Spirit. Anointing was also part of the burial procedures in Biblical times – as seen in the women who on Easter Sunday were on their way to anoint the body of Jesus. (See also **anointing the sick**.)

anointing the sick

The practice of the early Church, as part of their prayers for the sick, to place oil on a sick person as a visible sign of the prayer for healing. It also became associated with a preparation for death, when the prayers were offered 'in extremis'. The Roman Catholic and Orthodox Churches considered anointing the sick to be a sacrament, to be performed as a ritual by a priest. It came to be known as the Sacrament of 'Extreme Unction', also mistakenly called 'The Last Rites'. (See also **anointing**; **sacrament**.)

apocalypse or apocalyptic

A specialized style of literature which developed among the Jewish community during the years of the 2nd and 1st centuries BC. This was a time of severe persecution, making it necessary to develop a style of communication rich in symbolism, visions and dramatic images, often offered in the name of some great hero of Israel's past. It was a method of expression which allowed sacred coded words of encouragement and inspiration to be shared among a battered and disheartened people, undergoing persecution from their military conquerors. The specialized vocabulary of apocalyptic literature developed into a stylized format which allowed those within the tradition to share and communicate their hopes and dreams for the nation. The Book of Revelation in the New Testament is a much later example of apocalyptic writing – in this case, the expression of the Christian Church, persecuted by the Roman Empire. (See also **Revelation, Book of**.)

Apocrypha

Religious writings which, though earning a place in the Greek Old Testament, were not thought sufficiently reliable in terms of authorship, nor of high enough spiritual worth, to merit a place in the Hebrew canon of Scripture. Mostly written between 200 BC and AD 70, they represent a varied collection of historical, proverbial, religious, and moral stories. The Christian Church is divided as to the worth of the apocryphal writings. The Roman Catholic Church accepts them within its canon; the Anglican Communion allows them some status, but not to be taken account of when determining matters of doctrine. Apocryphal writings also vied for a place in the New Testament. They include several gospels, such as the Gospel of the Hebrews, and letters purporting to have been written by Paul. (See also **New Testament**; **Old Testament**.)

apostle

A title technically belonging only to the twelve disciples of Jesus (Judas Iscariot being replaced by Matthias) who were specially called to witness to his life and resurrection, and sent out by him as envoys of the gospel. Paul was added latterly to the list of those eligible to hold this special title, his particular mission being to go to the non-Jewish world with the good news of Christianity. In the history of the Church the title assumed a particular significance and authority, since those holding the title were regarded as having a special role and therefore their writings assumed a unique importance. Apostolic authorship guaranteed a place in the official canon of Scripture, as a result of which many books were written purporting to have this authorship. The term was eventually narrowed down to refer purely to the first twelve, plus Paul. (See also **disciples**.)

Apostles' Creed

An agreed statement of basic Christian beliefs widely used in both Roman Catholic and Protestant Churches as a refined crystallizing of essential doctrines. Highlighting the Trinitarian nature of God, it describes the work of God in creation, salvation, and sustaining power as Father, Son and Holy Spirit. Although originating as early as the 3rd century AD, it was not put into its present form until the 8th century.

archbishop

A bishop appointed to have responsibility for, and direction over, other bishops; often the head of a Province. In the Eastern churches there is a hierarchy of Archbishops. (See also **bishop**.)

archdeacon

Within Anglicanism, a clergyman given special responsibility for administration of all, or part, of a diocese, designated to his responsibility by the bishop, The role of archdeacon also existed within the Roman and Orthodox Churches, though it is no longer used by them.

Ark of the Covenant

A gold covered box, made of acacia wood, containing the stone tablets on which were written the Ten Commandments given to Moses on Mt Sinai. The top was decorated with two cherubim and was called the mercy seat. The ark was movable, with the aid of two special poles, and could be transported with the nomadic people wherever their travels took them. The Israelites carried it with them during their wilderness wanderings, but its normal place was in the very holiest part of the Tabernacle, the tent where God's presence was given to the Israelites. When the Temple of Solomon was eventually established, the Ark was placed in the innermost sanctuary, where it remained until Jerusalem was destroyed in 586 BC, and the people carried off into exile in Babylon. The Ark was never seen again, though a 1992 investigation has claimed its discovery in Ethiopia. (See also **mercy seat**; **Commandments, Ten**; **Tabernacle**.)

Armageddon

The location, referred to in the New Testament, of the last great battle between the forces of good and evil, God and Satan. The name may refer to a place by the mountains of Megiddo, in Israel. It may, however, simply be a symbolic representation of the idea of the ultimate victory of God's power over the dark forces ranged against him.

Arminianism

A theological stance developed from the teachings of the Dutch theologian Arminius (1560–1609), a follower of the reformer

7

Beza, and in his early thought a full-blown Calvinist. Arminius later shifted radically towards a doctrine of universal salvation – a view which ran counter to orthodox Calvinism and Reformed theology. The theological position of Arminianism was challenged at the historic Synod of Dort (1618), which reaffirmed with some force the traditional Calvinist doctrines of double predestination, original sin, total depravity, and the need for regeneration. Thereafter, Arminianism became a theology of the edges, with Calvinism holding centre stage in the processes of Protestantism. (See also **Calvinism**.)

Ascension

The technical term used to describe Christ leaving earth to return to his father (Acts 1.9–11). Although the word *ascension* is not itself used in the New Testament, the idea of being 'taken up' or 'lifted up' is present, emphasizing that this was a work of God, a further sign of God's vindication of his life, death and ministry. The Ascension is not as frequently occurring a theme as the Resurrection, and while the colourful language of the New Testament clearly carries with it a particular metaphysic – the idea of going *up* into heaven – the pictures used are primarily intended to express the truth that Christ returned to his position of glory and power in heaven. (See also **Resurrection of Jesus**.)

asceticism

The practice, within a variety of religions, of renouncing normal physical enjoyment and sensual pleasures. This renunciation was expressed through fasting, abstaining from sexual activity, meditation, solitude, hair-shirts, and the giving up of all possessions. All this, it was thought, would enable the devout worshipper to concentrate the mind wonderfully upon God without fear of distraction. (See also **monasticism**.)

ashram

A community of disciples in India, dedicated to living according to the teachings of a religious leader. They lived simple lives marked by self-discipline and restraint. The name derived from a Sanskrit root, meaning 'religious exercise'.

Ash Wednesday

The day which marks the beginning of the season of Lent – the forty days of meditation and preparation for the events of Easter. The name derives from the tradition found within the Catholic and Anglican Churches, whereby the branches used in the previous year's Palm Sunday celebrations are burned, the ashes being used to mark the sign of the cross on the forehead of the Christian. The ritual has its roots in the ancient practices of the Church. (See also **Lent**.)

Assumption

The tradition within the Roman Catholic Church that the Virgin Mary on her death was taken up into heaven, body and soul, without enduring the indignities of burial in the normal manner. It is a claim which derives from the logic of her unique personality as 'the Mother of God' rather than having any basis from within the Biblical accounts. (See also **Virgin Birth**.)

atheism

The denial of the existence of God, or indeed, of any gods. It is a view which broadens to include the rejection of any belief in supernatural powers, the conviction being that rationality requires a sceptical view of all claims about divine existence. Often atheism is justified on the basis that science or psychology can give rational accounts of phenomena or experiences usually cited by believers as grounds for their belief in the action of God. Atheists argue that, because the major tenets of religious faith are not susceptible to scientific testing, they are not sufficiently well grounded to merit serious attention. (See also **agnosticism**; **evolutionary humanism**; **theism**.)

atman /'ɑ:tmən/

The Hindu equivalent of the soul or true self. It is characterized by the teachings of the Upanishads as being of the same essence as the Absolute, and identified with Brahman. (See also **Hinduism**.)

atonement

A difficult but crucial element in Judeo-Christian concepts of sin and salvation. While in modern usage *atone* contains principally the idea of 'making up for our mistakes', the Bible's understanding is deeper and more wide-ranging. It belongs in the first instance to the world of the Jewish sacrificial system of the Old Testament, where the main idea is the need to put out of sight the sin that is so offensive to God. In the theology of Jewish ritual the lifeblood of the sacrificial victim (eg a lamb) is affirmed by God as having the power to atone for sin. This act is a vivid demonstration of the need for the sin to be obliterated, and a clear statement of the reality that the sinners themselves are incapable of putting things right by their own actions. Only God can put away sin.

In Judaism, the *Day of Atonement* (Yom Kippur) became an annual festival during which sacrifices were made to deal with the sin of the whole people. For the Christian faith, the atoning sacrifice of Christ himself, and his blood, provides the covering agency which obliterates sin. (See also **sacrifice**; **salvation**; **vicarious atonement**.)

Avatar /ˈævətɑː/

In Hindu thought, an appearance on earth in a visible form of one of the Gods, with a view to helping in some particular crisis. The tradition began with the God Vishnu coming to earth in human form, or sometimes as an animal, during a crucial moment of peril for the earth. (See also **Vishnu**.)

B

Baal /bɑːl, ˈbeɪəl/

A Canaanite god, the worship of whom by the native Canaanites constantly threatened to deflect the Israelites from the rigour of their own loyalty to the living God. Either by direct worship of Baal, or by adopting Canaanite religious practices, Israel was always in danger of allowing its true faith to be absorbed into that of its pagan neighbours. In the case of Queen Jezebel, there was a direct attempt by the rulers of Israel to introduce Baal worship. The prophets of Israel proved to be the champions of Judaism in its pure form.

Babylonian Exile

See **Exile, the**

Baha'i /bəˈhaɪ/

A religious movement emanating from an Islamic sect called the *Babi* in Persia in the late 19th century. The prophet of the Babi sect had spoken of the coming of a great prophet. This title was claimed by Mirza Husayn Ali, who called himself *Baha Allah*, 'the glory of God', and called people to his cause. His teachings emphasized the unity of God, and of all faiths, in the hope of the eventual unification of all humanity in harmony and peace, the fruits of universal education and good government. Local groups meet for informal worship in homes, and each member of the sect is assumed to be a teacher of the faith. There is no formal priestly order. There are Baha'i services for marriage, funerals and the naming of babies, but none of the stylized rituals associated with major faiths. The Baha'i faith has withstood much persecution, and still finds its adherents under pressure within intolerant religious regimes.

baptism

A ritual involving sprinkling with water, or the total immersion of the body in water. Although the Old Testament required specific types of water purification for hygiene and cultic purposes, baptism as such is a late development in religious practice. Those wishing to be received into the Jewish faith underwent baptism as an indication of ritual purification, while John the Baptist required of Jews that they be baptized as a sign of repentance and cleansing from sin in readiness for the coming Kingdom of God. In the Christian Church, baptism takes on a quite different theological importance. Converts, having confessed faith in Jesus, are baptized as a sign of entry into the Church. There is only a superficial resemblance to the baptism of John; the significance of Christian baptism is much deeper, effecting a kind of incorporation into Jesus Christ through a symbolic sharing of his death and resurrection. The ritual expresses the death of the old life of the convert and the beginning of a new life in Christ. (See also **conversion**; **purification**; **total immersion**; **water**.)

Baptists

A worldwide communion of Christians, who believe in the baptism only of believers prepared to make a personal confession of faith in Jesus Christ. They have certain links with the 16th-century Anabaptists, but mainly developed in England and Wales in the early 17th century, and later in the USA. Strongly biblical, the emphasis in worship is on scripture and preaching. Individual congregations are autonomous, but usually linked together in associations or unions. The Baptist World Alliance was formed in 1905. (See also **Anabaptists**.)

Bar Mitzvah /bɑːˈmɪtzvə/

For the Jews, a ceremony marking the achievement of the age of responsibility for males, reckoned to be 13 years plus one day. The tradition is that the young man will read from the Torah or the Books of the Prophets in the synagogue on the Sabbath, and is thereby recognized as a full member of the congregation with consequent privileges and duties. In non-orthodox synagogues, girls celebrate a *Bat Mitzvah* at the age of twelve years plus one day. (See also **Judaism**.)

Benedictines

A religious order committed to obedience to the rule of St Benedict of Nursia (c. 480–547 AD), who founded his order to pursue learning and scholarship. Each monastery was independent, but they were bound together by their common loyalty to

Benedict's Rule, which was drawn up to preserve the monks from the dangers of a wealthy self-indulgent existence. (See also **monasticism**.)

Bhagavadgita /bɑ:gəvɑ:d'gi:tə/
(Sanskrit, 'Song of the Lord')

A classic account in Hindu literature of the Hindu understanding of religion. It is a poem forming part of the great Hindu epic the *Mahabharata*, and tells the tale of a dialogue between the Lord Krishna, characterized as a charioteer, and a warrior prince Arjuna, on the eve of a great battle. The teaching contained in this basic sacred text has a profound importance for all Hindus: while there are many ways to salvation, they are not all equally appropriate. (See also **Hinduism**.)

bhakti /'bɑ:kti/
An attitude of loving devotion to God, prescribed in Hindu religious writings as the most effective way to reach God. As it involves a personal surrender, committed individuals, regardless of their earthly status, enjoy a personal relationship with God that is close and intimate. (See also **Hinduism**.)

Bible
A collection of 66 books covering a period of over 1200 years of religious reflection, discovery, insight and experience. The Old Testament writings were originally in Hebrew and Aramaic, while the New Testament was written originally in Greek. Although the Old Testament relates the struggles, triumphs, and pilgrimage of Judaism, it remains vital to the Christian Church, being seen as the root from which sprang a proper understanding of Jesus and the salvation he brings. All attempts to drive a wedge between the two Testaments have historically been resisted. The books represent a whole range of theological perspectives and understandings, yet they point to a consistent understanding of a God who involved himself intimately in the affairs of men and women, whose motivation is love, whose character is holy, and whose gift is salvation. (See also **Apocrypha**; **Canon of Scripture**; **form criticism**; **hermeneutics**; **higher criticism**; **New Testament**; **Old Testament**; **Pentateuch**; **redaction criticism**; **type**.)

bishop

A religious title which carries the sense of having charge over others, or of being an overseer of some kind. The New Testament seems to apply the term generally to those who had some sort of authority within the early Church – such as elders or presbyters, who were allocated positions of responsibility and leadership. Indeed, the roles of bishop and presbyter seem in the New Testament to be virtually interchangeable. It was not until the 2nd century that the current idea of *episcopacy* was developed, largely under the influence of Ignatius of Antioch – a hierarchical system of church government, where bishops hold the greatest authority. The Roman Catholic, Orthodox, and Anglican Communions have all consecrated bishops as the chief religious authorities within an area or diocese – with a cathedral as the mother church. Only bishops have the power to ordain priests and confirm baptized members of the Church. The pastoral oversight of all the clergy is in the bishop's care, as is the spiritual life of the whole diocese. (See also **apostle**; **archbishop**; **elders**.)

blasphemy

An insulting of God by a human being, seen as a sign of rebellion and resistance to the holiness and majesty of God. It can be an attitude born out of a commitment to paganism, and the rejection of God's authority by a heathen nation, or it can surface within the experience of the people of God themselves, when they act in such a way as to show disregard for his prerogatives. In the Old Testament it was punishable by death – so seriously did blasphemy challenge the whole fabric of the nation's life and the moral order on which community life depended.

blessing

An act which invites the goodness of God to rest upon someone. In its most primitive expression, blessing was considered to be an act full of magic and power – words which brought some good into being. In the Bible it came to be seen as something that only God could do, and thus gives a clue to his character and direction – the will he has inherent in his nature to convey good things upon his children. Blessing is usually expressed in a physical action, such as the hands being placed on the head, the act illustrating the meaning of the blessing as a gift of joy, life, and prosperity.

blood

A notion frequently used in the Bible in a symbolic way. It often highlights the seriousness of an arrangement or relationship such as the practice of becoming 'blood-brothers'. In religious ritual, blood is offered as the sign whereby communion between God and man can be restored. This was the purpose of the sacrificial system of blood-offerings, in which a lamb or a goat was killed and its blood used as a substitute remedy for the sin of the worshipper. These ideas are carried over into the New Testament, where the shed blood of Jesus is symbolized in the cup of the sacrament of communion, and constitutes a sacrifice of sufficient worth to 'wash away' the sins of the world. This theological understanding of the importance of blood explains the fierce ban on the eating of blood or bloody meats in Judaism. (See also **expiate**; **sacrifice**.)

bodhisattva /bədɪˈsætvə/

An element in Mahayana Buddhism whereby a person who has reached the state of enlightenment of a Buddha elects to remain in the world of human experience, sharing the enlightenment with others, rather than simply moving on to Nirvana. The enlightened existence brings to the human condition a spirit of charity and compassion in relation to social obligations and concern. This unselfish expression of love for others is a high point in Buddhism. (See also **Buddhism**; **Dalai Lama**; **Mahayana**.)

Book of Common Prayer

The official guidelines for orders of worship in the Church of England, used within the Anglican Communion worldwide. Largely the work of Archbishop Cranmer, it was first introduced in 1549 and later revised in 1552, 1604, and finally 1662. Highly regarded for its beautiful language, it has come to be viewed as a landmark in Christian expression, and a hugely appreciated aid to devotion. Attempts to update its language have met with mixed responses from among the faithful, and in its original form it continues to generate remarkable loyalty from traditionalists within the Anglican Communion. (See also **Anglican Communion**; **Church of England**.)

born-again Christian

See **evangelical**

Brahma

In Hindu religion, the creator God. Hinduism portrays a wide range of expressions of deity, Vishnu and Shiva representing different and contrasting elements of divinity. It is the role of Brahma to hold a balance between these two in a trinity (*Trimurti*) of deities. Brahma is the all-inclusive deity lying behind the many Gods of popular Hinduism. (See also **Hinduism**.)

Brahman

In Hindu thought, the eternal, impersonal Absolute principle. The name is an abstract, neuter form of Brahma, and expresses the idea of the cosmic unity of all things, the guiding principle beneath all reality. (See also **Brahma**.)

Brahmanism

A religion which dates from the Vedic period of 1200 to 1500 BC, and which is thought to have given rise to the great religious themes and traditions of Hinduism. Brahmanism was a religion of sacrifice and ritual, and recognized a special priestly class, dominant over all society, which took responsibility for the sacrificial cult and the preservation of religious thought and practice. The Brahmin class developed into an influential, powerful elite within society, emerging as the highest of the four Hindu social classes. (See also **Hinduism**.)

Brethren (in Christ)

A Christian Church, derived from the Mennonite tradition, founded in the late 18th century in Pennsylvania, USA. Initially it spread to Canada, and in a burst of international missionary activity founded congregations in Asia, Africa, and South America. Although in the 20th century its numbers are small, the zeal and commitment of its membership have given it an influence out of proportion to its size. (See also **Mennonites**.)

breviary

A book of material to aid devotion and encourage worship in the Roman Catholic Church. It contains psalms, prayers, hymns, and Bible passages for use within the daily devotional life of all clerics and priests. It was revised in 1971 by Pope Paul VI to take account of the significant changes made by the second Vatican Council. (See also **Office, Divine**.)

Buddhism

A world religion with roots in ancient Indian thought, based on the teaching of Buddha (Siddhartha Gautama (c. 563–c. 483 BC), believed to be one of a small but continuing series of 'enlightened' beings. The Buddha's teaching is gathered up in *Four Noble Truths*, the final one of which affirms the possibility of deliverance from the human experience of suffering by following a 'path'. A major theme is the law of *karma*, by which good and evil deeds result in rewards of punishments in this life, or a succession of rebirths. By obedience to the right path, human beings can break the chain of karma. Buddha's recommended path is morality, meditation, and wisdom – themes laid out in the *Eightfold Path*. The purpose of the whole exercise is to achieve *nirvana*, which is the blowing out of the fires of desire, and the absorption of the self into the infinite.

Even from its earliest days Buddhism divided into two main strands. *Theravada Buddhism* adheres firmly to the strict and narrow teachings of the earliest Buddhist texts, which call for severe discipline and effort in order to achieve salvation. *Mahayana Buddhism* is more liberal and takes account of the realities of popular piety. It teaches that salvation is possible for everyone, and it is from this strand of Buddhism that the idea of a personal saviour or *Bhodisattva* emerged. In both traditions, the basic thrust of Buddhism is to create an atmosphere conducive to spiritual development, leading eventually to deliverance from bondage to the limitations and suffering of this material and desire-orientated life. The disciplines of meditation and self-control are central to this process. (See also **Bhodisattva**; **Eightfold Path**; **Four Noble Truths**; **karma**; **nirvana**.)

burnt-offering

In Jewish ritual the burning of a young, perfect sheep, goat, bullock, or pigeon, after its blood had been sprinkled on the altar and the skin given to the priest. In cultic practice, burnt-offerings were made every morning and evening, and were seen as a symbol of the willingness of the worshippers to offer themselves without reservation to God in service and devotion. (See also **sacrifice**.)

C

call

See **vocation**

Calvary

(Latin 'skull')

The place outside the walls of the ancient city of Jerusalem where Jesus was crucified; also known as *Golgotha* (Aramaic 'skull'). The present day Church of the Holy Sepulchre is thought to have been built on the site of the original Calvary, but the precise location of the Crucifixion cannot be identified with any degree of certainty.

Calvinism

A Protestant Church deriving from the writings of the 16th-century Reformer John Calvin (1509–64). The term is not restricted to the actual theology developed by Calvin himself, nor even to the main doctrines of the 17th-century scholars who expanded his main themes under the title of the 'Five Points of Calvin' at the Synod of Dort (1618–19), but includes the main beliefs of those churches which grew up under Calvin's influence and became a distinctive and characteristic element in Reformed Church history. The key features of Calvinism are the sovereignty of God, the Bible as the supreme rule of faith, the much misunderstood doctrine of predestination, and a return to the New Testament doctrine of justification 'by faith alone'. A number of major 20th-century theologians, as a reaction against the liberalism of the late 19th century, have elected for the theological stance referred to as *neo-Calvinism*. (See also **Arminianism**; **Dutch Reformed Church**; **justification**; **predestination**.)

canonization

The process by which a deceased person is declared by the Roman Catholic Church to be a saint. It is a lengthy and protracted business, involving careful enquiries, with very specific require-ments needing to be met before status as a saint is confirmed. The benefits to the recipients of canonization include a special Festival Day of their own, the dedication of church buildings in their memory, and an enduring place within the ongoing history of the church. (See also **saint**.)

Canon of Scripture

The agreed collection of books held by the Christian Church to have been divinely inspired, and therefore authoritative in setting up ethical and theological standards. The gathering of the Old Testament into one volume of writing lies lost in ob-scurity, though it is clear that the books of the Law were the starting-point, being perhaps brought together under the influ-ence of Ezra. Indications are that by c. 140 BC the Law, the Prophets, and other writings were already in an agreed place of pre-eminence. The Greek translation of the Old Testament (the Septuagint) had between 250–50 BC itself made a selection. By AD 90 at the Synod of Janina, final decisions were made about books whose place in the accepted canon had been in some doubt (eg Esther and the Song of Solomon).

The collection of the New Testament canon is also a process about which little is known. The need for something to use in worship – and the death of immediate witnesses to the events of Christ's life – may well have encouraged the desire for a record that had some weight and authority within the church. This desire, plus the growing requirement to combat heresy and establish orthodoxy, explains the collection of the gospels, in the first instance, followed by Paul's letters, so that by 170, Iranaeus could assume a collection of 17 books. Later additions such as Hebrews and Revelations were some time in gaining acceptance, but by the Council of Rome (382) the agreed canon was complete. (See also **New Testament**; **Old Testament**.)

cardinal

A senior dignitary of the Roman Catholic Church – a priest or bishop nominated by a Pope to have special responsibility as a counsellor. Originally the title was borne by a parish priest, bishop, or district deacon of Rome. Cardinals are entitled to wear distinctive badges of office, such as the special red cap, or *biretta*. The duties of a Cardinal are largely to do with church administration – acting as head of a diocese, or being involved in an ecclesiastic commission, or a Congregation in Rome itself. When all the cardinals come together as a College, they hold responsibility for the Church of Rome during a vacancy in the papacy, and have since 1179 been responsible for the election of the Pope. (See also **Pope**.)

Carmelites

A monastic order within the Roman Catholic Church, originating in the 12th century, when the hermits of Mount Carmel in Israel sought to copy the way of life of Elijah the Prophet. Also known as the *White Friars*, they flourished as travelling beggars in Europe. Carmelite nuns became officially part of the order in 1452, and were re-formed by the mystic Theresa of Avila in Spain in 1562 as a cloistered order. St John of the Cross was responsible for re-forming the male order, and in 1593 an additional order of Discalced Carmelites was officially recognized. The older order emphasized teaching and preaching, while the Discalced order concentrated on practical and foreign mission work. (See also **monasticism**.)

catechism

A statement of Christian doctrine, in which the key teachings of Christianity are explained in a question-and-answer format for use as a teaching aid in the instruction of converts. It was used also at a later stage in a more developed and formal church setting for the instruction of those adults baptized in infancy, but ready to be confirmed within the life of the church. Catechisms came into wider use following the Reformation as a means of inculcating the principal themes of reformed theology – with Luther's 'shorter catechism' and the 'Heidelberg Catechism' being the most popular. The question-and-answer method was thought for many years to be an effective way of teaching, but recent educational trends have moved away from this approach, as seen in the Roman Catholic 'New Catechism' (1966), which dispenses with a dialogue format. (See also **Christianity**.)

cathedral

The main church of the bishop of a diocese. It was in the first instance the church which contained the bishop's throne;

later it was seen as the mother church of the diocese. Today the term is applied generally to any church of great size and significance. The great cathedrals whose marvellous architecture dominates several major European cities were in many places the focal point of community life and cultural expression. (See also **bishop**.)

Catholic

The word used to describe the universal or global reality of the Christian Church as a whole. The term is not used as such in the New Testament, but the idea pervades the various writings. Iranaeus in his Epistle to the Smyrneans is the first to introduce it to denote the general impact and efficacy of the church, spreading to every land and culture. The meaning altered during the development of Christianity towards the sense of 'orthodox' – the church that is faithful to the essential truth of Christianity. This emphasis is to be found chiefly in the Roman Catholic Church. However, this tradition also recognizes the relevance of the core meaning of *catholic*, referring to a kind of church which is to be found throughout the world, available for every sort of individual in the application of its message to all needs and all circumstances. (See also **Anglo-Catholic**; **Christianity**; **Roman Catholicism**.)

celibacy

An unmarried state, especially one in which the person voluntarily abstains from sexual intercourse. The concept is traceable to the teaching of St Paul, who saw sexual restraint as a way of demonstrating a dedicated and single-minded form of Christian service. The cult of celibacy was a familiar feature of Christian Church life from its earliest days, reaching its peak with the increased enthusiasm for an ascetic lifestyle among Christians. This attitude grew out of a reaction against the sumptuousness of secular life. The simple and restrained life of the committed Christian was set against the excesses, specifically the sexual excesses, of the secular world. Celibacy is still practised by members of both male and female religious orders in several beliefs, notably in the Roman Catholic Church.

chapel

Originally, a sacred place where holy religious relics were kept; later, any church building. In England and Wales the term is usually applied to nonconformist churches (eg Methodist and Baptist), while, peculiarly in Scotland and Northern Ireland, it refers to Roman Catholic places of worship. It is used technically in church architecture and liturgy to refer to the chancel – part of a cathedral where a special altar has been placed for worship by a small group of people.

charismatic movement

A movement of renewed spiritual energy and enthusiasm within contemporary Christianity, in which the emphasis is on the role of the Holy Spirit in awakening, reviving, and stimulating the Church, and the individual Christian. With a concentration on signs and demonstrations of the activity and presence of the Holy Spirit, it is often identified by the experience of 'speaking in tongues' and other spiritual phenomena not normally part of mainstream Christian worship. (See also **Holy Spirit**; **Pentecostalism**; **regeneration**; **tongues, speaking in**.)

cherub

A winged heavenly creature, a type of angel, referred to in the later books of the Old Testament. Often portrayed in the decoration of religious places, cherubs are found in sculptured form in the Tabernacle, set near the Ark of the Covenant, suggesting that a heavenly guard is being kept over the sacred items. A familiar feature of the mythology of other Eastern cultures, they remained an integral part of Jewish theology. Popular religious art has reduced them to rather clichéd representatives of God, in the form of shining round-faced baby-like creatures; hence the adjective *cherubic*, with its overtones. (See also **angel**; **seraphin**.)

Christadelphians

A Christian sect founded in c. 1848 by an American, John Thomas; also called the Brethren of Christ. It emphasized getting back to basic New Testament Christianity, with the conviction that Christ would come again very soon and establish a theocracy, the Kingdom of God on Earth, to last a thousand years. The sect has no official clergy; each congregation attends to its own worship and organization. (See also **millenarianism**.)

Christian

A title referring, in an ironic way, to the followers of Jesus. The first Christians preferred to call themselves the 'followers of the way', the 'saints', or occasionally 'the brethren'. The name *Christian* was first attached to them at Antioch by the Gentiles there, who used the familiar form of adding *-anus* after the name of a famous individual to denote those who were his followers. Thus, a name originally intended as a joke or jibe became a badge worn with pride by those committed to Jesus. (See also **Christianity**.)

Christianity

A major world religion, based on the life and work of Jesus of Nazareth, a Jew, believed by his followers to be the long-awaited Messiah of Israel, the anointed one, sent by God to be the Saviour – and to be in a unique relationship to God, whose Son he was revealed to be. After Jesus' death by crucifixion for the crime of blasphemy, his followers believed him to have been raised from death by God as proof of the truth of his message. He had declared the Kingdom of God, and had selected twelve disciples to be the bearers of the Good News (or Gospel) of this new Kingdom. The disciples preached and won converts, later committing the message of Jesus to writing – the New Testament as we have it being the account of the early days of the Christian Church. In spite of encountering fierce persecution, the Church continued to grow until in the 4th century Emperor Constantine made Christianity the official religion of the Roman Empire. While over the years it has been rent by schism, threatened by heresy, and opposed by oppressive rulers, it remains a hugely influential force in art, politics, and ethics – and continues to sustain the loyalties of men and women of all cultures.

For Christians the authority of the Bible is vitally significant; worship on a Sunday – the Lord's Day – celebrates the Easter memory of the Resurrection experience, while the obligation to compassion and love of neighbour is fundamental. Belief and practice are not to be separated in the Christian world view. A strong urge to share the good news of Jesus, the Saviour, drives the Christian Church to a missionary zeal, and explains the ongoing attempts to win the whole world for the Christian faith. This is done by persuasion, and while in less gentle times brutal methods were used, the error of that approach is now well recognized, and the spirit which dominates the Church today is one of love and compassion. (See also **apostle**; **catechism**; **Christian**; **Church of England**; **ecumenism**; **Gospel**; **New Testament**; **Orthodox Church**; **Reformation**.)

Christian Science

A Christian sect founded in 1879 in Boston, USA, by Mary Baker Eddy, its main theme being to re-establish the original Christian message of salvation from all evil – including sickness and disease, as well as sin. Mrs Eddy's book *Science and Health with Key to the Scriptures* (1875) was the influential, additional tool with which to interpret the Bible in harmony with the movement's main beliefs. A key belief is that, because God is a good creator, all our experience of the negative aspects of creation – disease, death, sin – must be the products of our own mistaken human viewpoint. Thus, health is enjoyed not by taking advantage of medical science (which Christian Scientists refuse), but by living the Christian life, and developing lives truly in tune with God. (See also **Christianity**.)

Christology

The technical term used by theologians to describe the scholarly discipline which tries to define and illuminate the nature of the person of Jesus Christ, in a way that is fitting, accurate, and adequate. Since Christ is absolutely central to the Christian faith, it is crucial for Christians to arrive at a proper understanding of who he was, and what his life and death were about. (See also **Christianity**.)

church

The English form of the Greek word *ecclesia*, which denotes the idea of a meeting or assembly of a community. It echoes the Old Testament picture of the people of Israel congregating for some common task or action. The idea of 'church' gradually developed the sense of holding an actual meeting, especially a service of worship; but more generally it simply refers to the Christian community, the people of God, wherever they might be. Various additional descriptions have borrowed ideas from the Old Testament to develop the notion: the church is seen as an 'elect race', a 'royal priesthood', 'a holy nation', and a 'new Israel', assuming the titles and responsibilities hitherto reserved for the Old Israel of Judaism. It has been called into being to proclaim and to live the Kingdom announced by Christ.

Churches of Christ

A Christian denomination founded in the 19th century in the USA, as a result of the work of Thomas and Alexander Campbell and Barton Stone. Its distinctive features are a firm rejection of all human creeds and confessions, and a desire to return to the simplicity of basic New Testament Christianity. A split occurred within the denomination which led to the formation of the Disciples of Christ – a group similar in belief but distinct from the Churches of Christ. (See also **Christianity**.)

Church of England

The national church of England, based on an episcopal structure, with the monarch officially as its head. It came into being when Henry VIII, in order to facilitate his divorce plans, and to gain control of the considerable wealth of the Roman Catholic Church severed connections with Rome, and had himself, rather than the Pope, declared the 'head' of the English Church in 1532. The Church of England retained many of the characteristic features of Roman Catholic worship until the reign of Edward VI, when more Protestant elements were introduced with the Book of Common Prayer (1549, 1552). Elizabeth I allowed an increasingly large Protestant element into the church, with the doctrinal statements of the Thirty-Nine Articles being noticeably more Protestant in tone. The swings between Roman Catholic and Protestant tendencies within the Church of England have persisted to this day, with the mixture being livened up still further by a new charismatic element, currently enjoying considerable influence.

The Church of England continues to hold a special and significant place within the international Anglican Communion, as the Mother Church of many congregations within the Commonwealth. There are at present 44 dioceses in the two provinces of Canterbury and York, with over 3000 churches and other places of worship. In 1970 the General Synod was formed to enable the Church of England to reach decisions and to express a common view on the issues of the day. (See also **Anglican Communion**; **Book of Common Prayer**; **Christianity**; **Reformation**.)

Church of Scotland

The national church of Scotland, which came into being at the Scottish Reformation in 1560, under the leadership of John Knox. It is charged with the provision of the ordinances of religion in every parish in Scotland. Some 1200 congregations are formed into Presbyteries (groups of congregations in a geographical area) which, in theory at least, determine church policy. Once a year, a General Assembly is held, where representatives of the Presbyteries form a final court of judgement, appeal, and decision. Lay men and women, in the shape of ordained elders, play a key part in the church's pastoral life and policy-making. While only ordained ministers, male or female, are allowed to administer the Sacraments, all major decisions relating to the life of the church involve the eldership – at local church level in Kirk Session, at Presbytery, and in General Assembly, where they are present in equal numbers to the clergy. (See also **Anglican Communion**; **Presbytery**.)

circumcision

The removal of the foreskin in men, and parts of the genitalia in women. A common practice in the Middle East and Africa, it may have originally been an initiation rite of some kind. In religious terms, circumcision is seen as an act of surrender, a sign of obedience towards God. In Judaism, it is the sign of the sharing in the covenant, which sets Israel apart as the people of God. In the New Testament, circumcision became a point of controversy within the Church, with St Paul being the champion of the view that the need for circumcision was over, as it was only an external demonstration. What counted for the Christian believer was the death and resurrection of Christ in the first instance, as the guarantee of salvation, and the inner faith of the believer. (See also **Judaism**.)

Cistercians

A religious order of monks, founded by Robert of Malesme at Citeaux in France in 1098, who lived by a strict rule which emphasized solitude, poverty, and a simple life-style. The order was influential in the Middle Ages and had among its leaders Bernard of Clairvaux. By the 13th century it had over 500 monasteries in Europe, but it gradually declined in influence, and by the 17th century it had split into several different styles of community. (See also **monasticism**; **Trappists**.)

cleanliness

A concept of ritual purity, important in many religions, towards which much of the effort of religious activity is directed. People can be *clean* or *unclean* – as can animals. Indeed, almost anything involved in religious life and activity, from the equipment used in cultic practices to the clothes worn by those engaged in ritual, can require to be rendered 'clean'. In Christianity, Jesus raised the issue of cleanness when he challenged the notion that externals were what counted, preferring in his view to look in the direction of true loyalty of heart towards God. However, much of what was involved in the practice of Israel's religion was conducted in order to assure ritual cleanness before the holiness of God. Uncleanness could be caused by sin, contamination by non-Jewish connections and influences, sometimes by sexual activity, contact with dead bodies, and any kind of rebellion towards God. It is dealt with in a variety of ways – by ritual washing, according to an agreed method, or by an effective sacrifice, the blood of which is sufficient in cleansing power to create the new status of 'clean'. (See also **purification**; **sacrifice**; **unclean meat**.)

clergy

The name given to those ordained or particularly set apart to carry out the work of religious bodies. They can be men or women, depending on the particular restrictions imposed by different religious groups. A wide range of titles is encountered, such as (within Christianity) ministers, priests, bishops, cardinals, vicars, rectors, deacons, and deans. (See also **monasticism**; **Orders, Holy**; **pastor**; **priest**.)

Commandments, Ten

The revealed Law and will of God, given to Moses on Mount Sinai, written on tablets of stone, and placed in the Ark of the Covenant, resident in the holiest place of the Tabernacle; also called the *Ten Commandments* or *Decalogue*. While other cultures had developed their own catalogues of ethical imperatives, the unique aspect of the Ten Commandments is the understanding that, by direct revelation of God, they bind God to the people; and the assumption is that they will be obeyed by a people who sense the privilege of their position. (See also **Ark of the Covenant**.)

Communion
See **Eucharist**

comparative religion
The examination from an unbiased position of the various religions of the world, to ascertain their distinguishing features and common elements. Using all the methods of objective study, comparisons are drawn not in any way to determine truth or validity, but to describe, analyse, and compare differences and similarities. The science is a recent one, and has revealed recurring patterns within religions, despite the separation of culture and distance. (See also **religion**.)

confession
(1)   A public affirmation of what is held to be true and believed with conviction. It is assumed by the New Testament that profession of belief is part of the normal Christian experience. What is felt in the heart is to be declared with the lips. Sometimes such confessions can have a structured form, the purpose of which is to establish norms of orthodoxy. Individual confessions can also be made, accepting a requirement, or expressing a desire to, conform.

(2)   The acknowledgement of sin, seen by the Bible to be a prerequisite of forgiveness and renewed communion with God. The refusal to acknowledge the 'disease' of sin removes the possibility of 'cure'. There is clear New Testament justification for the practice in some churches of Acts of Confession, for Christians are encouraged in the Epistles, in the interests of increased self-awareness and deepened trust, to be open with one another, even to the extent of confessing their sins to each other. In later church practice, this came to be formalized in the rite of confession before a priest, receiving the absolution he is permitted to offer in the name of Christ. (See also **forgiveness**; **penance**; **reconciliation**.)

confirmation

A Christian act of initiation, seen in some branches of the church to be a sacrament. It is a ritual at which individuals who have already been baptized, usually as children, and who have arrived at an age of personal responsibility, freely confess personal loyalty to the Christian faith. By their decision, they 'confirm' and lay claim to what was given to them in baptism, in a public profession of faith. The ritual takes the form of the laying on of hands, or anointing with oil, by a bishop. It was normal practice to be confirmed after the age of seven – though many churches prefer to postpone confirmation until adolescence, when a degree of mature understanding has been reached. (See also **bishop**; **laying on of hands**; **sacrament**.)

congregation

A gathering or assembly of the people of God, the community of faith. The term originally bore the sense of the people of Israel being distinct from other nations and especially designated as the people of God. For the New Testament, this idea is translated as 'church', in the sense of a particular gathering of believers in a single fellowship in a particular town or city. (See also **church**.)

Congregationalism

A body of belief within the Christian Church which prefers to use the model of the church as a *gathered* community of believers, committed to God, keeping his commandments, and accepting the rule of Jesus Christ over their lives. The roots of the movement lie in the separatists of the 16th-century Reformation in England, who broke away from the Church of England, considering its break with Rome was not radical enough. After persecution, they fled to Holland and later America – the Pilgrim Fathers of 1620 stemming from a congregationalist desire for freedom of worship. The form of church government and administration favoured within the movement sees the *local* church meeting as the decisive factor in making key decisions, the call of a minister, and general church affairs. This style has appealed to sufficient numbers to make Congregationalism a worldwide denomination, driven by a strong missionary emphasis, and strong commitment to principles of freedom of belief and tolerance. (See also **Reformation**.)

consubstantiation

Luther's attempt to describe the dynamics of the bread and wine of the Eucharist. The notion sought to retain the truth of the Real Presence of Christ in divine grace in the sacrament, while rejecting the Roman Catholic doctrine of transubstantiation, with its particular (and for the Reformers unacceptable) interpretation of what happens. Luther's solution was to speak of the presence of Christ 'under or with the elements of bread and wine'. He recognized that something special was available to the believer sharing in the sacrament, but wished to stop short of the Roman Catholic view that the bread and wine in some sense 'became' the body and blood of Jesus. (See also **Eucharist**; **transubstantiation**.)

conversion

A way of expressing a radical change of attitude and view, from stubborn error and rebellion against God to obedience, love, and worship. This occasionally dramatic change of heart is effected by the love and grace of God. Although the word appears only once in the whole New Testament, the idea is clearly basic to the evangelical thrust of the church's mission, with Saul of Tarsus and his dramatic 'conversion' on the road to Damascus a prime example. (See also **baptism**; **proselyte**.)

Coptic Church

An early Christian church, founded in Egypt (it is claimed, by St Mark), and numbering the great scholars and bishops of Alexandria among its early leadership (such as Clement of Alexandria and Athanasius the Theologian). It was early dogged by schism, and following the heresy of Monophysitism and the decisions of the Council of Chalcedon (451), it split from the rest of the Christian Church, confining its influence to Egypt. Arab invasions of the 7th and 11th centuries, attacks by the Turks, and the imposition of Islam in Egypt then seriously weakened its position. It still exists, using the ancient Coptic language, and preserving in its liturgy the Alexandrian forms of worship; but it has been somewhat marginalized by events.

cosmological argument

One of the traditional arguments which attempt to prove the existence of God. Its main thrust lies in the argument that, since everything in the world must have a cause, the Universe itself must have a cause, this First Cause being called God. Ingenious enough in its way, it never won widespread support within the world of philosophical thought. The law of cause and effect had itself only a dubious validity, and the argument begged the question of what is the cause of God himself. (See also **God**.)

Counter-Reformation

An attempt by the Roman Catholic Church in the mid-16th century to put its house in order, following the upheavals of the Protestant Reformation in Germany. The period following the Council of Trent (1545–63) saw a revival of the monastic movement and, more importantly, the creation of the new Order of the Jesuits. The idealism, however, was to be overtaken by a switch to the offensive, with the disciplinary measures of the Inquisition. (See also **Inquisition**; **Jesuits**; **Reformation**.)

covenant

A key concept in the religions of Judaism and Christianity. The basic notion is of a commitment entered into, a willingly undertaken binding of one to another, in a relationship that places responsibilities on each as well as bringing blessings and benefits. The world-shaking claim of the Bible is that God makes covenants with humanity. For example, he covenants with Noah that there will be no other destruction of the earth by flood, the sign of that covenant being the rainbow. He covenants with Abraham to be his God and to make his people a great multitude, the sign of that covenant being circumcision. And he covenants with the people of Israel at Mount Sinai, that he will be their God and they will be his people, the sign of that covenant being the Law of Moses, and the seal the sprinkled blood that is part of the ceremony. In its turn, Christianity is the religion of the 'new covenant', where Christ the Saviour inaugurates a fresh relationship as the Saviour of the world, the sacrament of bread and wine being the sign and the Holy Spirit the seal of this relationship.

While the basic ingredient of a covenant is the willingness of God to bind himself in eternal relationship to the recipients of the covenant-promise, the very clear expectation is that the recipients will in their turn respond in obedience, trust, and faithfulness.

Covenanters

Those who signed the National Covenant (1638) and the Solemn Oath and Covenant (1643) in Scotland, resisting the imposition of the principle of the divine right of kings on the government of church and nation. In Scotland, the movement had the added element of a rebellion against the episcopal system of church government which was being forced on Scotland's Presbyterian Church by the King. The Covenanters were declared rebels, and suffered persecution until the restoration of Presbyterianism in 1690. In the intervening years many were martyred, while others fled to refuge in Holland and the USA. (See also **Presbyterianism**.)

creation

The conviction that the world has come into being through the creative power and purposes of God, according to his plan and direction, and that the purpose of the exercise is to provide a context for mankind in the dignity of its freedom to love and serve God. As a theological conviction it stands in contradiction to any reductionist or materialist interpretation of reality as some kind of 'cosmic accident' or purely random natural occurrence. To accept the idea of creation is to see, without being too concerned with the details of the processes involved, that underlying everything that is, and sustaining it in existence, is the creative will of God, without whose decision to create there would be nothing. (See also **creationism**.)

creationism

Originally, the belief that God creates a soul for each new human being at conception or birth; now, the conviction that the Genesis account of the creation of the Universe it to be taken literally as a serious description of how things began. Creationism inevitably conflicts with the theory of evolution, but is nonetheless stoutly held by many of a conservative evangelical viewpoint. (See also **creation**.)

cult

A set of beliefs or practices associated with a particular god or group of gods forming a small but distinctive part of a larger religious movement. The focus of worship may be a specific object, place, or animal (as in the whale cult of the Eskimo region), a specific deity (as in the Shiva cult of Hinduism), or even a human being raised to the status of divinity (as in the emperor cult of Ancient Rome). Nowadays, cults tend to be deviations from mainstream religions, or entirely new religions gathered around the teachings of a particular leader. They have distinctive features, such as a strong emphasis on discipline and obedience to the leader or group, though this can result in unwelcome control over the individuality of the cult follower. (See also **religion**; **sect**.)

curate

A Christian clergyman permitted to enjoy the role of the 'cure of souls' and having the charge of a parish. However, the term is popularly applied to an assistant or unbeneficed clergyman, whose job is to help (or temporarily replace) the priest, rector, or vicar of a parish. (See also **clergy**.)

D

Dalai Lama

The religious and political head of Tibet, believed by his followers to be an incarnation of the Bodhisattva Avalokiteshavara. The present Dalai Lama, Tensin Gymatso, born in 1935 and thought to be the fourteenth incarnation, ruled in Tibet from 1940 to 1959, fleeing to India as a result of an uprising. Awarded the Nobel Peace Prize in 1989, he is still regarded by Tibetans as their spiritual leader. (See also **bodhisattva**; **Lamaism**.)

deacon, deaconess

A lower tier of ministry within the early Christian Church. The ministries take various forms, but all of them are subject to the leaders within the church community. The precise definition of areas of responsibility is not clear, but the idea of service of a *practical* kind seems clearly implied, in examples discovered within the life of the New Testament Church. As church administration grew more complex, a specific order of deacons and deaconesses began to emerge, and still serves as an auxiliary ministry of service.

Dead Sea Scrolls

Manuscripts hidden by members of the Jewish sect of the Essenes at Qumran, near the Dead Sea, and discovered in 1947. The find was particularly exciting to archaeologists because it supplied them with around 500 documents, many in fragments, but some in good condition, containing Hebrew versions of almost all the Old Testament scriptures. The scrolls were almost 1000 years older than any manuscripts of the Old Testament hitherto available to scholars. (See also **Essenes**; **Qumran**.)

dean

In Christianity, a senior clergyman in a cathedral, chapter, or diocese. The roots of the office lie in the monastic tradition, where a dean was originally an experienced monk in charge of ten (Latin *decem*) novices.

'death of God' theology

A brand of theology which sought to reduce the transcendent and supernatural elements in Christianity, presenting it instead as a rational system of beliefs about the uniqueness of Christ and his teachings. It emerged in the 1960s as an attempt to make Christianity palatable in a scientific age. Influenced by Hegel, Nietzsche, and Bonhoeffer, its main champions included American theologians, William Hamilton (1924–), Paul Van Buren (1924–), and Thomas Altizer (1927–). (See also **theology**.)

deism

Belief in the existence of a god or gods; specifically belief in the existence of a supreme being who, though the basis and source of all existence, stands back from the world he has made, and lets it get on with its own existence. The term came to refer also to a particular strand of British religious thought of the 17th and 18th centuries, which laid emphasis on the possibility of discovering God from the evidence of the natural order he has created – without depending on special revelations to arrive at truth. (See also **theism**.)

demon

A spiritual entity or force determinedly arraigned against God, seeking to frustrate and destroy his purposes. The ancient gods of pagan religions were considered to be demonic, while Satan himself, set in every degree against God, was thought to have his agents of evil destructive power. In the New Testament, the association between disease and possession by demons is clearly stated, and evidence for the healing powers of Jesus was demonstrated in his power and authority over demonic influences. Psychiatric practice would seem to challenge this simple identification of mental or emotional disorder and demonic possession, yet the expelling of evil spirits from the life of the 'possessed' (*exorcism*) has remained a practice of the Church, and it may be too simplistic to dismiss as purely psychological every experience of demon possession. Along with belief in a Holy Spirit and the possibility of a 'spirit-filled life', there is the logical possibility of a life given over to worshipping the spirit of evil. (See also **Satan**.)

demythologizing

A critical process identifying a 20th-century school of thought, led by the German theologian, Rudolf Bultmann (1884-1976), which claims that the only way to explore the meaning of the Bible is to adopt an existentialist approach. Borrowing much of his existentialist philosophy from the German philosopher Martin Heidegger, Bultmann argues that Christians must push past the obvious *literal* meaning – with its cultural presuppositions and pre-scientific view of the world – to find the underlying truths which can move an individual to decision, commitment, and action. When the stories of the Bible are stripped to their bare essentials of meaning, and the ancient categories of fable, myth, symbol, and allegory are cut back, so as to expose the heart of the 'message for me', then – the argument runs – individuals are in touch with its true purpose, and can uncover its real meaning. (See also **Bible**.)

devil

See **Satan**

dharma /'dɑ:mə/

An idea from Hindu thought which has a wide variety of meanings, important within Hinduism. It is fundamentally the law of the universe which underpins everything. As a moral law, it applies to the whole of society and with particular force to each individual, regardless of social status. (See also **Hinduism**.)

didache /'dɪdəkeɪ/

A short handbook of Christian moral teaching, with guidelines for church administration, dating from the 2nd century AD. The full title is 'the teaching of the Lord through the twelve disciples'. Its importance lies in what it tells of the way in which the early Church was ordered, what its sacramental practices were, and its methods of ministry.

disciples

People who meet to listen to the teaching of scholars, rabbis, intellectuals, and other respected figures. In the case of Jesus, there was a 'two-tier' system of disciples: the inner circle of the Twelve, with special privileges and responsibilities; and fringe followers, for whom discipleship operated on the edges of commitment. The unique feature of Jesus's call to discipleship ('follow me') is that it was a call to *personal* loyalty, not simply intellectual assent to the truth and validity of his teaching. (See also **apostle**.)

dispersion

The migration of the Jews from Palestine to towns and cities throughout the world, as a result of famine, war, or deportation, in particular at the time of the Exile to Babylon. It was an important influence on Judaism for various reasons: it exposed Judaism to a whole range of cultural influences; it created a network of world Jewry; and it generated a notion of Return, of the flock of God being brought home into the safety of the sheepfold of Israel. It also created the dramatic backcloth for events around Pentecost, as the Jews of the Dispersion returned home for the great Festivals. 'Next year, in Jerusalem' became a powerful dream for the dispersed and homeless Jews. (See also **Judaism**; **Pentecost**; **Zionism**.)

Dissenters

Those who refuse to accept a consensus viewpoint, and decide to break away from the main body of opinion. Within Christianity, the Dissenters were a very specific group, who chose to separate themselves from the established or national church in the 17th century. Also known as Nonconformists, they insisted on the right of individual Christians to find their own forms of worship and their own shape of church government. (See also **Nonconformists**; **Reformation**.)

divination

Finding out the truth, or unpacking the future, by special consultation with a god. The Old Testament disapproves of the practice, and while it is clear that God does use dreams and visions as vehicles to express his revelation, soothsaying, astrology, and superstition were proscribed, introducing as they did elements that seemed to the Old Testament writers to undermine trust in God's power to see through his purposes to the end. (See also **occultism**.)

dogma

An agreed, authoritative position on a crucial item of belief. In religion, it is usually the conclusion of centuries of theological debate on what constitutes essential doctrine. In Christianity, dogmas are the result of the Church seeking to interpret the meaning of the Bible, distilling its teaching on such key matters as the person of Christ and the Trinity.

Dominicans

A religious order founded in 1216 by St Dominic (c. 1170–1221) to defend the Roman Catholic faith. Devoted to preaching and teaching, the Order accepts the discipline of poverty, and has produced some fine scholars and theologians including Thomas Aquinas and Albertus Magnus. Now a worldwide movement, it has a sister order of nuns, and also a non-enclosed order. (See also **monasticism**.)

dove

A symbol of gentleness, peace, and tenderness, introduced during hard times in Israel as an acceptable form of sacrifice to be offered by the poor. In the book of Genesis, the dove is seen bearing the olive-branch – a harbinger of peace and reconciliation between God and man. Its symbolic significance was radically reinterpreted at the baptism of Jesus, when it appears as a sign of the presence of the Holy Spirit. Following that incident, the dove became a visible symbol of the Spirit within the life of the Church. (See also **Holy Spirit**.)

Druze

An Islamic faith, an off-shoot of the Ismailis, which originated during the closing years of the Fatimid caliph al-Hakim (AD 996–1021). They deviate considerably in belief and practice from the main Muslim body, teaching mystical ideas about emanations from God being experienced by devotees, and awaiting the return from divine concealment of al-Hakim and his disciple Hamza ibn Ali. The Druze are found chiefly in Syria and Lebanon. (See also **Ismailis**.)

dualism

In religion, a theory of an eternal principle of both good and evil in the human condition, with the spirit representing the good element, and physical nature the evil. It originated within Greek philosophy, and influenced the Church through the teachings of Gnosticism. Christian theology rejects dualism because it allows evil an independent integrity and eternal existence, which runs contrary to the Christian notion of evil as partial and contingent – the absence of good and the denial of God. (See also **Gnosticism**.)

Dutch Reformed Church

The largest Protestant denomination in the Netherlands, originating in the Calvinist Reformation in the 16th century. Its theologians and leaders have enjoyed a respected place in Dutch life and in the framing of reformed thought worldwide. It should be distinguished from the Dutch Reformed Church of South Africa, a quite separate church seen for many years within the world community as a bastion of white supremacy. The South African Church was condemned by other reformed churches for its attempt to justify apartheid on theological grounds, as well as for pursuing the philosophy in its practice. (See also **Calvinism**.)

E

ecumenism

The genuine desire to express and discover visible unity between the divided churches and denominations within Christianity. It is a trend, growing within the mainstream churches, to lay aside ancient feuds and prejudices, and to emphasize and rediscover common truths. The ecumenical movement resulted in the formation of the world Council of Churches in 1948, as well as several national Councils of Churches, working to encourage genuine creative dialogue between their members. (See also **Christianity**; **Taizé**; **World Council of Churches**.)

Eden

The mythological garden where the story of mankind began. Fertile and perfect, it represents all the promise, potential, and hope enshrined in the human spirit, and lost through rebellion against the will of God. There have been attempts to locate Eden, using clues from the Book of Genesis, but its true significance lies not so much in whether it lies in the region of Mesopotamia, in a region watered by the rivers Tigris and Euphrates, but in what it stands for as a symbol of paradise lost, a testimony to the power of sin to rob and destroy.

Eightfold Path

The fourth of Buddha's Four Noble Truths, prescribing the way to arrive at Enlightenment. The ingredients of the Path include right understanding, right aspiration, right speech, right conduct, right means of making a living, right endeavour, right mindfulness, and right contemplation. (See also **Buddhism**; **Four Noble Truths**.)

elders

Originally, men of experience and wisdom within the community of Israel, held in high esteem within the life of the nation. For the

New Testament, they are understood as leaders appointed within the local church to positions of oversight and responsibility. The roles of elder and bishop in the New Testament church seem to have been indistinguishable from each other. In the Reformed Tradition, ordination to the role of elder remains the highest office available to the lay person, and indeed ordained ministers are considered chiefly to be 'teaching elders', an idea no doubt devised to keep them in their place, free from any unhealthy delusions of grandeur!

elect, the

People chosen or set apart through divine favour. The idea is widespread in the Bible, though the word *election* is infrequent in translations. The Children of Israel were, in the first instance, seen to be 'chosen' by God for no other reason than it was his will to move from the smallness and insignificance of Israel, to his global plan for creation. Sometimes the mantle of election falls on particular individuals, such as Abraham, David, or one of the prophets, who enjoy the dubious privilege of special status because they carry the often uncomfortable burden of particular responsibilities in the service of God. In the New Testament, the notion of election persists, with the Church now constituting the elect, and facing a similar range of responsibilities to serve as witnesses to the gospel and channels for the spirit of God. In some theological stances, the notion is given a twist which creates a different interpretation.

In this form, while some are chosen to serve and witness, others are not so chosen, and must by implication face election to damnation, eternal loss, or whatever the obverse of salvation is thought to be. However, the idea of God specifically preordaining people to eternal destruction would generally be considered alien to the whole thrust of the gospel. (See also **salvation**.)

encyclical

Originally a specific letter addressed by the Pope to churches in a particular area; now an official letter containing instruction of a doctrinal or pastoral nature issued by the Pope to the whole of the Roman Catholic Church. The assumption is that, once issued, its instructions will be followed. (See also **Pope**.)

ephod /'i:fɒd/

A linen apron, worn by the priests of Israel, fastened over the shoulder and usually highly decorated with ornate designs. The High Priest's ephod was a garment of particular richness, and carried considerable spiritual significance as an article of religious vestment. (See also **vestments**.)

episcopacy

See **bishop**

eschatology

A branch of religious belief to do with the last things – how God will bring his plan for creation to its fulfilment and decide the final destiny of each individual. It specifically concerns such notions as death, judgement, hell, and heaven. Within Christian theology, it is an element where there seems to be an endless appetite for lunatic-fringe interpretations of the Bible, and preoccupation with times and places, far removed from the true concerns of eschatology. The early Church, however, seems to speak of the return of Christ (the 'second coming') in largely symbolic language: as the world had a beginning, so it will have an end, with the victory of love over sin and death, and the glory of God revealed for all to see. (See also **religion**.)

Essenes

An ascetic scion of Judaism, dating from around the 2nd century BC until the 1st century AD, which opted for a simple community life. The Essenes came together in monastic groups, well away from the main centres of culture and life, as a sign of their outright rejection of the corruptions which they saw in Temple worship. They were severe in their abstemious life-style, often refraining from marriage, rejecting all possessions, and seeking the pursuit of a holy life. It is thought possible that John the Baptist had strong connections with the sect, and that Jesus himself maintained friendships with them. The discovery of the Dead Sea Scrolls at Qumran, and the excavations of the community based there, gave exciting new insights into the nature and religious philosophy of the Essenes. (See also **Dead Sea Scrolls**; **Qumran**.)

Eucharist
A Christian sacrament in which people partake of bread and wine as a commemoration of the death of Christ; also called *(Holy) Communion.* It derives from the Greek word for 'thanksgiving', and emphasizes the joy of the worshipper, who celebrates the Good News of salvation, forgiveness, and eternal life. The cup of wine becomes the cup of celebration and victory, the worshipper receiving a foretaste of the celebration feast of heaven, spoken of by Jesus at the Last Supper. (See also **consubstantiation**; **Last Supper**; **transubstantiation**.)

evangelical
A name within the Christian Church for someone who emphasizes the importance of making a personal decision for Christ, usually involving a conversion experience; colloquially known as a *born-again Christian.* Evangelicals insist on the authority of the Bible in all matters, interpreting this work literally as the inspired Word of God, and generally holding views representing a narrow theological conservatism. A distinction needs to be drawn between evangelicals, in this sense, and those belonging to theologically more liberal churches who are nonetheless driven by a concern to preach the Gospel and win converts for Christianity. (See also **evangelist**; **fundamentalism**; **witness**.)

evangelist
Originally, a writer of any of the four Christian Gospels; thus, anyone who spreads the gospel by preaching outside or inside the Church. The term comes from Greek *evangelion* 'good news'. The function has persisted throughout the story of the Church, and while some self-proclaimed American 'evangelists', with their colourful private lives, have tended to bring the integrity of the function into disrepute, the role has proved to be remarkably persistent in each generation. (See also **Gospel**; **mission**; **preaching**.)

evolutionary humanism
The view that, since modern scientific discoveries and the knowledge available to mankind have now liberated people from dependence on supernatural notions and religious dogma, there is no need to depend on religious moral codes or interpretations

of existence that require God. There are no hidden meanings, and there is no special significance to human existence. Science, harnessed to human reason, will bring about the goals men and women seek, and help humanity evolve towards a higher level of insight and achievement. (See also **atheism**.)

Exile, the

A crucial, epoch-making experience for the people of Judah, when the cream of the nation were deported to Babylon, following the fall of Jerusalem in 586 BC; also called the *Babylonian Exile* or *Captivity*. This was a time when the very existence of Judaism was threatened. Into that period of loss and sadness, the prophets (such as Ezekiel) came with their messages of hope and faith, calling the people to a renewed awareness of the power and promises of their God, and generating in exiled Jews the hope of a return to Judah and Jerusalem. The exile formally ended in 538 BC, when Cyrus the Great gave the Jews permission to return to Palestine. (See also **Judaism**.)

existence of God

See **cosmological argument**; **ontological argument**; **teleological argument**

Exodus, the

The escape by the Hebrews from Egypt, and their journey to the 'promised land' of Canaan, under the charismatic leadership of Moses. Although Pharaoh had been reluctant to accede to Moses's historic request to 'let my people go', a series of severe plagues and pestilences persuaded him to allow the people to leave. It is believed that these events occurred in the 13th century BC during the reign of Rameses II. For Israel, the departure and deliverance were events of fundamental importance, delivering the people from bondage, and setting in motion the whole history of Israel. The events continue to be celebrated in Judaism in the annual Passover Meal, recalling the night of hurried departure and the deliverance made possible by the power of God. (See also **Judaism**.)

exorcism

See **demon**

expiate

A technical term in Biblical thought which expresses the idea of the removal of sin or of the problem that sin causes between people and God. In the Old Testament, sin was thought to be so indelible that people could do nothing by themselves to remove the obstacle between them and God. However, through the mercy of God, the blood of a sacrifice is allowed to serve as the expiation to remove the stain of sin. (See also **blood**; **forgiveness**; **propitiation; sacrifice**.)

Extreme Unction

See **anointing the sick**

F

faith

Humanity's way of responding to the love and promise of God. It subsumes the notion of a proper response of obedience to God, and the belief that the prime mover in that relationship is God, who gives it substance and direction. Thus, in the Old Testament, the people of Israel as a community are required to respond in faith to God, and individuals are also expected to trust in the certainties of God's character and word. In the New Testament, Jesus is the one who calls men and women to faith in him. Faith in this sense has little to do with interesting reflections about his life or teaching, but a real personal *engagement* with his summons to 'follow'. The notion has developed negative associations, stemming from rationalist criticism, which seem to threaten its intellectual integrity; for example, such phrases as 'blind faith' or a 'leap of faith' seem to suggest some kind of loss of rationality. On the contrary, faith can be reasoned and mind-broadening, and it is interesting to notice that in the New Testament it is not moral depravity that is the ultimate evil, but impiety, or lack of faith – an attitude the New Testament considers to represent an attempted annulment of all God's purposes. (See also **faith healing**; **vocation**.)

faith healing

The process whereby sickness or mental illness is cured – or at least alleviated – by the ministry of a healer drawing power from a higher, supernatural source. Through the faith of the recipient, this source is able to work with healing power, and bring about physical or psychological improvements. Many of the world's religions have a place for faith healing within their beliefs – often part of their worshipping life. The practice has increased in recent years within the Christian Church, as a feature of the charismatic or Pentecostal stream of expression. It is normally interpreted as the work of God's miraculous power channelled through the open door of a believing heart; but some understand it to be merely a psychological process, simply explained as a demonstration of the mind's power over the body's chemical processes. (See also **faith**.)

Fall, the

A frequently used term to describe the first rebellion from God's way, which requires obedience, and mankind's subsequent deterioration into sinfulness. The Biblical account tells of mankind's removal from the primordial innocence of the Garden of Eden, and of the tragic inclusion of the whole of creation in the consequences of the fall from grace. The Genesis story of Adam and Eve reworks ideas from different ancient mythologies to produce a story rich in religious symbolism and theological power. Its clear message is that sin sets in motion consequences of dreadful seriousness, and that when freedom of decision is abused, disaster follows. (See also **original sin**; **salvation**.)

fasting

The practice of abstaining from food, and sometimes also water, in order to experience a heightened religious feeling, demonstrating particular piety, and reinforcing the seriousness of prayers. It is a common feature of many religions. In the Old Testament it could be practised by the community as a whole in times of particular crisis, or by individuals keen to take their religious life particularly seriously. It was often a sign of sadness or grieving, and was required, in particular, as part of the experience of the Day of Atonement, when the sins of the whole people were being 'dealt with' by the High Priest. In the New Testament, the practice also occurred, Christ himself fasting on one occasion for 40 days and nights. Because his concern was not chiefly about the externals of religious observance but on the inner piety of faith in God, he seems to have imposed no pattern on his followers of a requirement to fast. Nonetheless, Christians throughout the history of the Church have adopted fasting as a spiritual discipline and an adjunct to serious prayer. (See **Ramadan**.)

Fathers of the Church

The first theologians of the Church, the original Christian writers and thinkers whose task was to interpret the Bible account of the life of Jesus and draw out the implications of that life. Initially, Christian doctrine was little more than a series of Bible texts and affirmations, but this soon developed into a literature of considered reflection and scholarship. The study of the thought and writings of these early theologians is *patristics*. (See also **Roman Catholicism**.)

feminist theology

A response to the inadequacies apparent in the male-orientated thought processes and non-inclusive language found in traditional theology. Feminist theology attempts to redefine traditional theology, in order to take account of the religious needs, experience, and contribution of women – seeking out symbols, images, and models which recognize the special experience of women, and their religious, social, and cultural self-consciousness. (See also **theology**.)

festival

A time of celebration, usually marked by a special meal, or gathering of the community, inspired by a particular historical event or religious theme. For Israel, there were three main festivals in the year: the Passover, the Feast of Weeks, and the Feast of the Tabernacles. Harking back in origin to ancient agricultural festivals with no special theological meaning, these festivals developed into times of reflection and recollection of important religious themes. The Feast of Passover, on the third day of the first month, took the form of a joyful recollection of the great event of the Exodus from Egypt. The Feast of Weeks was also thought of as the Feast of Harvest, or Pentecost. It came 50 days after the offering of the first sheaf, and signified the end of a successful harvest. It also came to assume religious overtones as a celebration of the giving of the Law to Moses. The Day of Atonement was a more solemn experience, preceded by fasting, and this was the occasion when the sins of the people were dealt with in due ceremony through the offices of the High Priest. The Feast of Tabernacles came at the end of the harvest, and lasted seven or eight days, during which time the Israelites lived in shelters made of fronds and leaves to recall the days of their wilderness journeys under the leadership of Moses.

In the New Testament, some of these feasts are reinterpreted, in the light of the experience of the Church. The Passover is overshadowed by Holy Communion, and Pentecost becomes the feast of the Holy Spirit, the day the Christian Church was born.

Five Pillars

See **Islam**

flesh

An idea used to remind humanity of its humanness – a pejorative term which indicates the physicality of human nature, and the reality of weak earthbound existence. It is with the full awareness of this rather negative assessment of humanity that the New Testament insists on affirming the truth that 'the word became flesh and dwelt among us': the eternal freedom and truth of God, immune from and apart from all that is weak and inadequate, became 'flesh' with all its weakness, limitations, and corruption.

forgiveness

A crucial concept in the understanding of Old Testament and New Testament religious ideas, expressing the need to mend the breakdown in the relationship between people and God which has come about as a result of sin. The revelation of the Bible is that forgiveness mends this breach in relations, and that the act of forgiving sin is God's prerogative and gift. For the New Testament, forgiveness is linked to the life and work of Jesus. Christian believers, in their turn, are required to demonstrate in their own situation an attitude of generosity of heart and a forgiving spirit. (See also **atonement; reconciliation**.)

frankincense

A sweet-smelling substance used in the production of incense, traditionally burned as a symbolic gesture of worship. It is best known from its mention in the story of the birth of Christ, as a gift brought by one of the wise men. It would have been recognized by the Gospel readers as a special indication of the divinity of the child, and therefore of the uniqueness of the miracle of his birth. (See also **worship**.)

form criticism

An important school of Biblical scholarship, which seeks to iden-tify particular passages of the Bible according to the form in which they are written (eg miracle stories, pronouncement stories), and categorizes them accordingly. It sets similar passages together, so that their common roots can be clearly seen, and uses this information to reach a fuller understanding of how the Bible came to be compiled. A basic assumption is that the writings of the New Testament emerge from the needs of the early Church, and reflect its life and faith, at least as much as giving an accurate account of particular events. The stories were told within the Church, it is suggested, to encourage and inspire, rather than to inform about actual events – and thus, it is concluded, the issue of historical accuracy was not one which gave the early Church much concern. (See also **Bible**.)

Four Horsemen of the Apocalypse

Four characters, on horses of different colours, described in vivid symbolic language in the Book of Revelation in the New Testament. Their arrival symbolizes the end of the world, and the devastation which will accompany that event. The black horse represents famine; the red horse bloodshed and war; the pale horse, pestilence and death; and the white horse, the power of God triumphantly conquering the forces of wickedness. (See also **Revelation, Book of**.)

Four Noble Truths

The essential ingredients of the teaching of Buddha: all life involves suffering; the cause of suffering is craving or desire; there is an escape from suffering, because craving and desire can end; the Eightfold Path brings about the end of suffering and sorrow. (See also **Buddhism**; **Eightfold Path**.)

Franciscans

A religious order founded by Francis of Assisi in the early 13th century, as a reaction against the increasing wealth of the existing religious orders within the Roman Catholic Church. It has over the years divided into various groups, each with its own particular emphasis, such as the Friars Minor, Observants, Conventuals, and Capuchins. Their main work involves preaching to the poor and needy. A second order consists of nuns known as the Poor Clares, and a lay fraternity makes up a third order. Franciscans now constitute the largest religious order in the Roman Catholic Church. (See also **monasticism**.)

friars

Professional religious beggars, who travelled Europe seeking to support their religious devotions on the strength of the charity of others. A familiar sight in the Middle Ages, they did not attach themselves to a particular monastery or abbey. In spite of the rather romantic view which is found today, contemporary records reveal that they were regarded by many as nothing more than a nuisance.

Friends, Society of

A Christian sect, more popularly known as *Quakers*, founded in mid-17th-century England by George Fox (1624–91). The name 'Quakers' stems from Fox's instruction to 'quake at the Word of the Lord'. Persecution of the group led William Penn to establish a Quaker colony in 1682 in the USA. The basis of Quaker worship is the belief in the inner light within individuals which makes possible a living contact with the Divine Spirit. Silence is a major ingredient in their worship – where friends gather and wait upon one of their number being moved by the Spirit to speak. They seek simplicity in all things, and are strong champions of tolerance, justice, and peace.

fundamentalism

An expression of Christianity which seeks to preserve and promote what are considered to be the fundamental doctrines of the Christian Faith. The term was first coined to describe the conservative Protestant movement in America in the 1970s, where a key ingredient was an insistence upon the literal truth of the Bible and the firm refusal to countenance the critical approach of modern biblical scholarship. The term has since come to be applied to any conservative Christianity with a theology opposed to liberalism. In America it has also come to be associated with a particular stance – the Moral Majority – led by a number of preachers who represent a powerful force within American political life. The appeal of fundamentalism lies in its willingness to provide certainty, to give answers, rather than engage in the exploration involved in asking hard and searching questions. The same attitude of mind can be recognized among other world religions, and the term is now widely used for any zealous and jealous regard for the 'fundamentals' of a religion, such as within Islam and Judaism. (See also **evangelical**.)

G

Gabriel

An archangel, one of the top echelon of God's heavenly messengers. He appears in the Book of Daniel to clarify a vision, and in the New Testament tells Elizabeth of the forthcoming birth of John the Baptist. It is also he who comes to Mary with the message that she is to bear a child conceived by the Holy Spirit. (See also **angel**; **Annunciation**.)

Gehenna

A valley just outside Jerusalem, which because of its history became a symbol of decay, destruction, and the very curse of God. Kings had offered human sacrifices to the pagan god Moloch there, and the valley had also been defiled by Josiah. It served as a dump, where refuse and the corpses of criminals and animals were buried. The constant smoking fires of Gehenna came to serve as a symbol of the fires of hell, and this idea is taken up and developed by the New Testament. It figures as the archetypal place of judgement, eternal punishment, where burns the 'unquenchable fire'.

General Assembly

The highest court of the Church within the Presbyterian form of Church government. Made up of equal numbers of ministers and elders, it usually meets once a year to determine the policy of the Church and to serve as the last court of appeal on matters relating to Church law and practice. It is presided over by a Moderator, who acts as chairperson and spiritual adviser, and who is elected annually. (See also **Presbyterianism**.)

Gethsemane /gɛθ'sɛmǝni:/

A location on the slopes of the Mount of Olives close by Jerusalem, used by Jesus as a retreat – a place where he prayed with and for his disciples, and where he was arrested after his captors had been led there by the treacherous disciple, Judas Iscariot.

Gethsemane has become a symbol of the internal anguish that was very much part of the sufferings of Jesus.

Gideons International

An international organization committed to spreading the message of the Christian faith through the distribution of copies of the Bible in a whole range of public places, such as hotels, hospitals, and military bases. It began in Wisconsin in 1898, taking its name from the great leader of Israel, Gideon. Supported by committed Christian businessmen all over the world, the Gideon Bible, with its helpful guidelines, is a familiar sight to travellers. (See also **Bible**.)

glossolalia

See **tongues, speaking in**

Gnosticism /'nɒstɪsɪzm/

A heresy which grew up within the early centuries of Christianity; the term derives from the Greek word for 'knowledge'. It claimed that salvation was dependent upon access to secretly-revealed knowledge about existence, the origins of the world, and the nature and destiny of the human soul. Later forms of Gnosticism spoke of this secret knowledge being imparted by a heavenly redeemer figure. Its oblique and contrary view of the nature of the Creator God and of the person of Christ led to an inevitable collision with the orthodox faith of the early Church. (See also **Mandeans**.)

God

The living being believed by the Old and New Testament writers to be the source and creator of all things. He reveals himself to humanity in order to win loyalty and love, and in his moral authority is the one who judges the destiny of all. In Jewish and early Christian theologies, there is no need to explain or persuade people about the existence of such a being of ultimate significance. The existence of God is taken as given, it being inconceivable to Jew and Christian alike that any other explanation of existence could sustain the weight of reality as it is experienced. It is only in later years that philosophers have felt the need to justify God's existence.

God, as understood in the Bible, has particular characteristics to indicate his uniqueness or supremacy over the other 'gods' of paganism. He is a living being, not an idol carved out of stone or fine metals, and is presented as having emotions, responses, expectations and hopes. He is described as the only true God, who jealously insists on his rights and prerogatives, and calls for ultimate and exclusive loyalty from his creatures. He is also seen as a God who takes a great interest in the lives of men and women, shaping history to his ultimate purposes, and highlighting the importance of the divine-human dialogue. It is to make this connection enduring and possible that God, in the Christian view, becomes still more intimately involved with the human predicament, coming to the world in the person of Jesus of Nazareth.

By describing Jesus as the 'Son of God' and allowing to him functions hitherto reserved only for God himself, the New Testament clearly indicates a qualitative difference between Jesus and any of the prophets of Israel's history. Indeed, for the New Testament he is properly understood only as the complete revelation of the previously hidden God. The whole thrust of Christian theology, and the unequivocal conviction of the Christian faith is thus to affirm the divinity of Jesus Christ. The experience of the Church at Pentecost, when the promised Holy Spirit was poured out across the life of the Church, drove Christian thinking to a Trinitarian understanding of God. The underlying energy in all of this is love. The New Testament declares that 'God is love' and to experience love is to experience God – the Bible's richest insight. (See also **Allah**; **Bible**; **existence of God**; **Trimurti**; **Trinity**; **Yahweh**.)

Golden Rule

The popular name for the saying of Jesus recorded in the Gospels of Matthew and Luke to the effect 'do unto others as you would have them do unto you'. While there is nothing radically new in this ethical view (it is found in earlier Greek and Jewish thought), popular religiosity has come to see this as a major ingredient of Christian faith.

Golgotha

See **Calvary**

Gomorrah /gəˈmɒrə/

A city of serious moral decay and decadence, destroyed by fire and brimstone, according to the Book of Genesis. Along with its neighbouring city of Sodom, it came to be a symbol of depravity and wickedness. Positioned in the Valley of Siddim, now submerged beneath the waters of the Dead Sea, the devastation that struck it became a sign of warning about the dangers of unrestrained corruption.

Gospel

A term from Old English, meaning 'good news', referring to the account in the New Testament of Jesus Christ and the Kingdom of God which he brings into being. The Gospel is the happy declaration that God has acted in the coming of Jesus to demonstrate his love and to bring salvation and forgiveness to all. The term was only used much later to refer to the writings which tell the story – the Gospels of Matthew, Mark, Luke and John. (See also **evangelist**; **New Testament**; **Q**; **Social Gospel**.)

grace

A key idea in New Testament Christian thought, which seeks to convey the sense of the generous love of God, leading to his undeserved action on behalf of humanity in order to put right the broken relationship between them that mankind's sin and rebellion have caused. The doctrine of salvation by grace shifts the emphasis away from any human agency, and lays the whole achievement of salvation on the heart of God and his love. This direction was emphasized at the Reformation, where the drift away from grace to ideas of 'salvation by works' was halted by Luther, and the miracle of God's sheer love was re-affirmed. (See also **salvation**; **sin**.)

guilt-offering

An important sacrifice in the Jewish cultic pattern, which originated before the time of the Exile. It grew in importance within the ritual as a way of dealing with sins committed unknowingly, or with those committed in respect of personal property. Once a sin with regard to property was acknowledged, a lamb or ram had to be sacrificed and an offering of one fifth of the value of the sacrifice had to be given to the priests. When this offering was accepted the sin was considered covered and the offence forgiven. (See also **sacrifice**.)

Guru

Within Hinduism a spiritual teacher or guide who gives instruction to a disciple or pupil. The pupil in turn treats the Guru with an appropriate reverence and obedience. In Sikhism, Guru is identified with the inner voice of God, of which the Ten Gurus of Sikhism were the human instruments. (See also **Hinduism**; **Maharishi**; **Sikhism**.)

H

Hadith /hə'diːθ/

A body of Islamic teaching and tradition on a whole range of subjects, second in authority as a guide for living only to the Koran. Finding its origins in the teaching of the Prophet Mohammed, or one of his companions, it contains an account of its own pedigree, its authority being traced back through a long series of validated sources. (See also **Islam**.)

Hare Krishna movement

A religion which seeks to promote human welfare by encouraging 'God consciousness', inspired by the ancient Vedic writings of India. The chanting of mantras is an integral part of their approach to worship. They are also committed vegetarians, refuse intoxicants, do not gamble, and live celibate lives other than for procreation within marriage. The movement was founded in 1965 in the USA by His Divine Grace A C Bhaktivedanta, Swami Prabhupada, as the International Society for Krishna Consciousness. Its shaven-headed, saffron-robed devotees are a familiar sight in the streets of big cities. (See also **Veda**.)

Hasidim /'hæsɪdɪm/

Those Jews in the 2nd century BC who resisted the Greek and pagan infiltrations of Israel's religion, and insisted on strict adherence to the Jewish Law; the name derives from Hebrew, meaning 'faithful ones'. They are probably the forerunners of the Pharisees of the New Testament. Supporters of the Maccabean Revolt, they later declined to fight for national independence until the legitimate priesthood had been restored. Out of that root came *Hasidism*, a feature of modern Jewish life, with its own historical origins in a popular Jewish mysticism developed in a persecuted Jewish sect in Poland in the 18th century. The characteristic forms of Hasidism include strict adherence to the Law of Moses, loud ecstatic worship, and a simple, ascetic lifestyle. Although initially at odds with traditional Jewish practices and the whole Rabbinic structure of modern Judaism, it spread throughout Europe and eventually came to be accepted as an aspect of Orthodox Judaism. (See also **Judaism**.)

heaven

A term with a variety of senses, ranging from the physical to the symbolic. In the first sense it reveals the way the Bible thought the universe operates, where the idea of a three-decker universe reflected the idea of heaven lying above the world of earthly preoccupations, with the dark world of the dead and its stark uncertainties beneath. In the theological sense, it identifies the realm of the supernatural, where God reigns supreme and from where he despatches his messages, and watches over his creation. Heaven is also the hope of Christians who consider themselves, in the words of the New Testament, to be 'citizens of heaven', no less than a creature bound by this world's shifting moods. In this context, heaven represents a realm of peace and celebration where, together with his children, God will celebrate the victory of Jesus and the triumph of love. (See also **hell**; **Paradise**.)

Hegira /ˈhɛdʒɪrə/

An important event in the life of the prophet Mohammed, his migration from Mecca to Medina in AD 622. The event marked the beginning of the Muslim era. (See also **Islam**.)

hell

A word used to translate the Old Testament word *sheol* and the New Testament word *hades*, which express the notion of a place where the spirits of the dead go. The Old Testament did not develop a serious view of life after death until quite late in the progress of its thought, tending to see survival after death as being located in the children born to an individual. Christian theology developed the notion as a place or state to which unrepentant sinners go after this life – often (especially in art) depicted as a place of fire and torment. Much contemporary Christian thought rejects the idea of vindictive punishment as incompatible with belief in a loving God. The emphasis accordingly shifts from hell as a place of retribution to a state of being without God. (See also **heaven**; **limbo**; **perdition**.)

heresy

A belief which deviates from the agreed norms of orthodox religious faith, specifically associated with the development of Catholic Christianity. False doctrine, or the denial of the truth of agreed elements within the corpus of Christian belief, is viewed by the Christian community as unacceptable, requiring a change of viewpoint if the punishment of excommunication is to be avoided. In certain times and countries, heresy has been considered a crime liable to the severest punishment. (See also **Pelagianism**.)

hermeneutics

The principles and methodology of Biblical study and interpretation. The subject has its origin in Greek philosophy, which sought to find a way to establish the true meaning of a text; and this discipline gained new energy when, in the 18th century, the problems posed by Biblical interpretation required the development of an acceptable strategy for dealing with the material. A whole variety of methods was suggested to handle the complex issues of cultural difference, the passage of time, the intentions of the writers, the historical context of the authors, the intrusion of personal preferences, and cultural blind spots, raising vital issues of social science, linguistic analysis, and textual criticism. (See also **Bible**.)

higher criticism

An approach to the study of the Bible which sought to free scholarship from the restraints imposed by the requirement to treat the work as so sacred that normal investigative and critical criteria could not be applied to its examination. Those who espoused the methods of higher criticism were unimpressed by generally held assumptions about the time of writing of particular books, the place where the books were written, or suppositions about their purpose. They wanted instead to be liberated from such preoccupations, and to examine the literature of the Bible using all the techniques and skills that would be applied by serious scholarship to any ancient text. This approach met resistance from those who saw such a secular handling of sacred books as an exercise which could seriously undermine faith. (See also **Bible**.)

high places

Shrines or places of worship used by pagan nations for the worship of their heathen deities. Confusions arose when the places so used, high hills or suitable places underneath trees, came to be taken over by the Jews and used for worship of the Lord. Despite rededication, these places continued to carry the associations of earlier cultic practices, and time and again reformers within Judaism challenged their use. They were abolished altogether during King Josiah's reforms, when worship was entirely focused on the Temple in Jerusalem. (See also **worship**.)

High Priest

The chief member of the ancient Jewish priesthood, inaugurated by Aaron in the Old Testament. Prior to the upheavals of the Exile it was likely that each local place of worship in Judaism would have its High Priest, who would function within ritual as the mediator of the sacrificial system. However, by the exilic period, the High Priest developed as a national functionary, with a unique role as a mediator for the whole people. He represented the twelve tribes of Israel before the Lord, and was the only one permitted to enter the innermost sanctum of the Temple, once a year on the Day of Atonement. In the New Testament, the notion of High Priest is applied to Jesus, seen to act as the representative of mankind, not in the partial way of the High Priest of the Temple, but through the power and perfection of his own life. (See also **Judaism**; **Levites**; **priest**.)

Hinduism

A religious tradition developed over several thousand years in India, subsuming a diversity of forms and practices which disallow any simple definition of its essential nature. Hinduism seems to have evolved without reference to any one great leader or teacher, or one special book, into a dominant cultural, social, and religious force within Indian life. A Hindu can worship a god, no god, or several gods, can use quite different sets of holy scriptures from another Hindu, and participate in quite different sets of festivals and rituals. Yet, because their religious convictions are concerned with a particular view of life and death, there are vital common elements – in particular the belief that how people live, shapes the nature of their next life, into which they will be reborn.

The theology of Hinduism is a complex one, but the centre-point of their notion of the divine is the Trimurti, a triad of Gods – Vishnu, Shiva and Brahma – accompanied by loyalty to a series of minor deities. Inspirational writings called the Vedas support the ideology which underlies these convictions, while temples, rituals, pilgrimages and festivals, overseen by the priestly Brahmin class of Indian society, dominate Hindu religious life and practice. (See also **Bhagavadgita**; **Brahma**; **Brahmanism**; **Trimurti**; **Veda**.)

holy

When applied to God, a characteristic purity, freedom, and integrity which separates him from the realm of weakness and approximation that is our human experience. God's holiness is a fierce and fearsome quality, from which people shy away or hide, because it represents a bright illumination of truth, exposing the sins of humanity. Although the original sense of the word has to do with something or someone being set apart for particular veneration or significance, it came to develop moral overtones of purity – a purity that is to be respected and preserved from contamination. Thus, places or things can be holy, insofar as they are especially designated for some function within the ritual of worship. And certain individuals are also designated holy, because of their particular intimate connection with God, or with the special tasks or equipment of cultic life. The people of Israel are recognized in the Bible as a holy people, in the sense not so much of achieved moral perfection, but of being set apart for the special task of revealing the will of God to the world. It is also a title assumed by the Church as the 'new Israel', a special people cut out for the crucial role of witnessing to the gospel of Jesus. (See also **Holy Spirit**; **sanctify**; **worship**.)

Holy of Holies
See **Tabernacle**

Holy Orders
See **Orders, Holy**

Holy Spirit

The third person of the Trinity in Christian thought; also called the *Spirit of God* or *Holy Ghost*. The work of God in creation is seen as being realized through the spiritual power and dynamism of the spirit of God. The birth of Jesus, the power that lay behind his mighty works, and the sustaining energy that kept his mission on track, are all understood to be the work of the Holy Spirit, as is the transforming courage found by the post-resurrection disciples following Pentecost, and the martyrs of the early Church. (See also **God**; **Pentecost**; **spirit**; **Trinity**.)

hope

An important idea which recognizes the complexity of human experience, and the fact of time as a reality with which faith has to deal. The experience of hope is an ongoing fact of life for believers. Because they cannot possess the future in the present, and because 'promise' is a key theme of Biblical faith, the experience of waiting in faith for the fulfilment of the promise is that experience of hope. For the Bible, the basis of this hope is the God who has demonstrated his reliability in the past, who sustains the believer in the present, and who can be confidently trusted in the future to do what he says he will do. Christian 'hope', which comes into its own in the face of death, has been a sustaining inspiration to acts of supreme courage, and a willingness to endure martyrdom, throughout the history of the church.

hosanna

A word of rejoicing and faith, a cry for blessing derived from the Hebrew word meaning 'save (us)'. Often used at harvest festival worship in Israel, it resounded with particular force during the Palm Sunday procession, as Jesus led the cheering crowds into Jerusalem – an incident which has brought the word to the attention of a wide audience.

hymn

The use of poetry and song in praise of God. Hymns are found throughout the Old Testament, and it is clear that they were often sung accompanied by musical instruments of various kinds. Prayer was gathered up and expressed as song, and the Temple worship came to include choirs and professional musicians. The Psalms were the main diet of sung praise, though a number of hymns do appear in the New Testament; and it is clear that hymn singing was a common feature of the worship of the early Church. Hymn writing and singing persisted as the common practice within Christianity, and came to be significant agents for the expression of Christian devotion throughout the centuries. (See also **Psalms**.)

I

icon

A representation of Christ, the Virgin Mary, various saints, or even important events in sacred history; the term is derived from the Greek word for 'image'. Icons have been used since the 5th century to help worshippers in their acts of devotion. Mostly found in the Greek and Russian Orthodox churches, they have a recognizably Byzantine style – flat, painted in oils on wood, and frequently very ornate, with elaborate decorations of gold and silver. They are believed to be sacred opportunities to enjoy God's blessing.

iconoclasm

The rejection of all images, or the veneration of them. An extreme view, based on the Ten Commandments' injunction 'not to make any graven images', it has had a wide range of supporters, including occasional Popes, the Roman Emperors of the 8th century, and strict Protestant Reformers of the 18th century. The notion has since come to be applied to an attitude of mind which opposes *any* established attitude, hero, or socially-agreed consensus.

idolatry

The practice of making tangible representations of deities. Common among the peoples of the ancient world, idolatry was abhorred by the religion of Judaism, going as it did against the commandment 'not to make any graven images', and challenging the uniqueness of the one true God. Indeed, the idea of bowing down to idols made out of stone, wood, or even precious metals, is viewed by the Old Testament as a ridiculously inadequate substitute for the worship of the living God. Notwithstanding the prohibitions, from earliest days the physical reality of an idol, and the ease with which it could be worshipped, held an ongoing attraction for the people of Israel, who kept requiring to be recalled by prophet, priest, and occasionally king to the purity of the worship of Yahweh. The desire for something tangible as a focal point of worship has been a continuous need for religious people, and various aids to devotion – crucifixes, icons, statues, stained-glass windows – have all sought to give some kind of visual expression to the fundamental truths of Christianity. However, these should not be confused with idols.

Imam /ɪˈmɑːm/

A religious leader and teacher of a Sunni-Muslim community, charged with leading worship in the Mosque. The name has also come to be applied to an especially influential and charismatic leader among Shi'ite Muslims. According to their faith, the line of Imams ended in the 9th century, and since then the Ayatollahs serve as a kind of collective leadership, caretakers together of the office until the longed-for reappearance of the last Imam. (See also **Islam**.)

Immaculate Conception

The belief that the Virgin Mary, from the moment of her conception, was free from sin – a doctrine defined by the Roman Catholic Church in 1854 in order to address the question of how a truly sinless Jesus could be born of a human mother. The doctrine has always been considered by Protestants to be unbiblical and unnecessary, and it was also rejected by the Orthodox Church after 1854.

Index Librorum Prohibitorum

('Index of Forbidden Books') The list of books which Roman Catholics were forbidden to read, originating in AD 496, and last revised in 1948. While the Roman Catholic Church retains the right to forbid its members from reading material which is considered harmful to their faith or morals, it was decided in the relaxed mood of 1966 to publish no further editions.

Indra

In Hinduism, described in the Vedic Scriptures as the King of the Gods. Many of the prayers found in the classic texts of Hinduism are specifically addressed to Indra. (See also **Hinduism**.)

indulgences

Special grants of remission of sin to the living, on repentance, and also to the dead in purgatory. The Roman Catholic Church in the Middle Ages believed itself to have accumulated a treasury of merit, built up through the centuries, and based on the good works of Jesus and the saints of the Church. The practice of selling indulgences, and of buying and selling places in heaven, was one of the serious abuses practised by the Church at that time, and led to Luther's protest against the direction in which the Church had drifted. It is too much to say that indulgences *caused* the Reformation; but their promotion, the theology which lay behind them, and the corruption which accompanied them, were major factors in prompting the Reformers to take action. (See also **Reformation**.)

infallibility

The claim of the Roman Catholic Church that statements made by the Pope, while speaking *ex cathedra* ('from the throne') on matters of faith and morals, or by a general council if confirmed by the Pope, are guaranteed to have been assisted by the Holy Spirit, and are therefore to be considered free of error. The doctrine was defined in 1871, and has been consistently rejected by Protestants, who insist that only God and the Word of God can be considered infallible. (See also **Pope**.)

Inquisition

A special tribunal drawn up for the prosecution of heresy, originating in the medieval Church. In the 13th century, Pope Gregory IX gave special authority to Papal inquisitors to counter the threat of political and religious rebellion from heretical groups. The sinister overtones associated with the term derive from the extremes of cruelty and torture for which the institution came to be notorious. The most infamous was the Spanish Inquisition, which continued to have influence until the 19th century. (See also **heresy**.)

inspiration

In theology, divine influence which allows a person to receive and communicate sacred revelation. The discussion has centred on the extent to which inspiration is present in the writing of the Bible. Were the writers precisely and in every detail dictated to by God, so that they were simply mouthpieces, recorders of the divine word? Or was the inspiration more in the way of other inspired work, such as poetry or music, where the skills, insights, and personality remain ingredients of what appears in the final work? The issue remains controversial with Biblical fundamentalists, who maintain a strict notion of scriptural infallibility, comprising an important group within contemporary Christianity. (See also **Bible**; Scriptures.)

Islam

A monotheistic religion, founded in the 7th century AD by the prophet Mohammed (also spelled Muhammad). Its fundamental requirement is obedience to the command of Allah as laid down in the sacred book, the Koran. The Islamic assumption is that the teachings of the Koran will pervade the whole of the committed Muslim's life and culture, and the demands are strict and unwavering. The Five Pillars of Islam define the life of faith: prayer, five times a day; witness to the truth as revealed in the Koran; alms-giving; fasting; and, if possible, pilgrimage to the holy city of Mecca. The teaching of Islam recognizes the role of other great 'prophets', such as Moses and Jesus, in the revelation of the will of God; but Mohammed is someone very special, holding a unique role as the one to whom the greatest of all books, the Koran, was revealed.

While there is no professional structure of priesthood, descendants of the Prophet, and holy men within Islam (such as mullahs and ayatollahs), have a significant role in the preservation and promotion of the faith. Its two main groupings are the Sunni Muslims, who look to the four caliphs who followed Mohammed as the legitimate heirs to the truth of the faith, and the Shi'ite Muslims, who look to the 'Imam' as the authority within the religious life of the Muslim. Emerging at a time when the Arab world was beginning to develop a sense of unified identity, and having within its religious philosophy the doctrine of *Jihad* ('holy war'), its expansion in the name of Allah was rapid and effective. The upsurge of Islamic fundamentalism, and the Muslim republics of the Arab and African worlds, indicate that the vibrant discipline of Islam is still a potent force in world affairs. (See also **Allah**; **Imam**; **Jihad**; **Koran**; **Pillars of Islam**.)

Ismailis /ɪzˈmaɪliːz/

Adherents of a secret Islamic sect, one of the main branches of
the Shi'ites; also known as the 'Seveners'. The sect developed
from an underground movement in the 9th century, reaching
political power in Egypt and N Africa in the 10th–12th centuries.
It distinguished between inner and outer aspects of religion, was
critical of Islamic law, and believed that in the eventual new age
of the seventh Imam a kind of universal religion would emerge
that was independent of the laws of all organized religions. Thus it
welcomed adherents of other religions, but retained its own secret
traditions and rites. (See also **Imam**; **Islam**.)

Israel

The new name given to the ancient patriarch Jacob, after an
encounter with God in which he 'struggled' with the Lord. The
precise meaning of the name remains lost in antiquity, but it was
passed on to Jacob's descendants, and the twelve tribes which
emanated from them. During the early years of the settlement
in Canaan, the name came to be associated with the northern
kingdom, as distinct from Judah in the south. In 721 BC the
northern kingdom fell to the Assyrian Empire, and the area was
colonized by foreigners. Following the exile of the elite class in
the southern region, the name was assumed by the remnant left
behind, who saw themselves to be the true children of Israel, and
in time Israel became the generic name for the Jewish nation.
The name is also claimed by the members of the early Christian
Church, who saw themselves as heirs of the promises given to
Israel and as the ones who had acknowledged the coming of the
Messiah. (See also **Bible**; **Judaism**.)

J

Jainism

A religion native to India which looks to Vardhamana Mahavira (599–527 BC) as its founder, believing him to be the last great hero (*Tirthankara*) within its tradition. Jains consider that overcoming material existence is the way to salvation, which calls for extreme self-denial and asceticism. By this means the soul can be released from the working of karma to enjoy all-knowing bliss. Detachment from worldly preoccupations is the prerequisite of liberation; and central to that notion is the practice of non-injury to living beings. (See also **karma**; **Tirthankara**.)

Jehovah

An attempt to explain in English the Hebrew sacred name for God, YHWH – a word which was considered too sacred ever to be uttered. Combining the sacred initials with the vowels of the substitute word *Adonai* resulted in the form YAHWEH, and *Jehovah* is a late Latin rendering of the Hebrew form. In English Bible translations, YHWH is given as *Lord* or *God*. (See also **Yahweh**.)

Jehovah's Witnesses

A religious movement which places particular emphasis on the last days and on the millennium of peace that will be inaugurated by the second coming of Christ.

Founded in 1884 in the USA under the leadership of Charles Russell (1852–1916), the members were at first called 'Millennial Dawnists', but adopted their present name in 1931. Using their own particular translation of the Bible, which they interpret literally, they anticipate the imminent second coming of Christ, and pledge their primary loyalty to the Law of Christ. They refuse to take oaths in court, to do military service, or receive blood transfusions, and they are legendary for their resolute door-to-door preaching methods. (See also **millenarianism**.)

Jesuits

A religious order, founded in 1540 by Ignatius De Loyola (c. 1491–1556) to support the work of the Roman Catholic Church during its action in the Counter-Reformation; properly known as the *Society of Jesus*. It is a strict and disciplined order, committed to Ignatius's Spiritual Exercises, and pledged in special loyalty to the Pope. It has developed a reputation for its brilliant thinkers and its academic achievements, founding colleges and universities throughout the world. The order has a broad-ranging, missionary aim, involving itself in a variety of approaches to ministry. It has proved to be a leading resource of rigorous and loyal apologists for the Roman Catholic Church. (See also **Counter-Reformation**.)

Jesus

See **Christianity**

Jew

A name originally used specifically for those who were Judeans, living in the southern kingdom and later applying to Judeans during and after the exile to Babylon (586 BC). By New Testament times it came to refer to all descendants of the people of Israel who espoused the religion of Judaism. (See also **Judaism**.)

Jihad /ʤɪˈhæd/

In Islam, the concept of a 'holy war'. The Koran calls on Muslims to oppose those who reject Islam – if necessary by force – and this has built into the thinking of Islam an aggressiveness which explains its triumphant march in many parts of the world. The Jihad has been invoked to justify Islam's militarist expansion, and its effort to defend itself. Islamic states still apply the justification of the idea of Jihad, and the Muslim world declared a Jihad against Israel in the Mecca Declaration of 1981. (See also **Islam**.)

jinja /ˈʤɪnʤə/

A small Shinto shrine or sanctuary. It is sometimes by a roadside, sometimes a larger building in the centre of a group of smaller buildings. It can also be a large group of temple buildings with a wooded area around it. The central feature is the main dwelling of the deity, which has a single room in which the sacred symbol is kept. (See also **Shinto**.)

Job

Part of the writings of Israel designated as wisdom literature, which attempts to explore the mystery of innocent suffering. Using dramatic narrative, the Book of Job examines the bewilderment of Job, a devout man whose life is upended by calamity after calamity. Dated somewhere between the 7th and 3rd centuries BC, it expresses a dualism which is a later development in Jewish thought, with Satan being given limited powers by God to test the resilience of Job's faith. The drama is reinforced by the introduction of 'Job's comforters', friends who gather round to explain to him why all these disasters have befallen him, and why basically it must be his fault. (See also **faith**; **wisdom**.)

Jordan, River

A river of practical, theological, and poetic significance in the story of the Bible. Three streams come together above Lake Hillel, flow into it, then out down a narrow valley into the Sea of Galilee. From here it flows south along a winding basin to end 1200 feet below sea level at the Dead Sea. So crucial a geographical feature soon had military, economic, and social effects, which in turn developed religious overtones and meaning. First it proved a difficult and intimidating boundary to be crossed by the fearful Hebrew people in order to lay claim to the Promised Land of Canaan. Challenged by Joshua to demonstrate faith and courage, the children of Israel finally 'crossed that Jordan River', and settled in the Promised Land. Its cleansing powers were seen as both physical and spiritual, Naaman the leper being healed there, and John offering baptism there as a sign of repentance. In Christian imagery 'crossing the Jordan River' came to symbolize the necessary passage through death before the Promised Land of heaven could be enjoyed. As a consequence, this river is a frequent image in hymns and Christian art.

Judaism

The monotheistic religion of the Jewish people, whose belief is that the one true living God, the creator of all things, specially chose the people of Israel to be a witness to his nature, and to communicate his will to all the world. By equipping them with the special insight and revelation of his Law, given to Moses on Mount Sinai, he established them as his people who would be the channels of his self-disclosure. The Hebrew Bible is a key resource for Judaism, telling the story of God's dealings with his sometimes faithless people, and the constancy of his commitment to the ancient covenant he had made with them, that he would be their God and they would be his people.

Since the destruction of the Temple in Jerusalem, synagogue worship is the normal pattern of religious devotion, while special festivals, recollecting great moments in Israel's history, are an ongoing element in its liturgical life. A strong ethical foundation and concern, a tremendous sense of a crucial connection with a past where God has been, and a general affection and respect for family life as a sacred trust are the key ingredients in a religion which has endured prejudice and persecution beyond imagination. (See also **Ark of the Covenant**; **Bar Mitzvah**; **Bible**; **Circumcision**; **festival**; **Israel**; **Law, the**: **rabbi**; **synagogue**; **Tabernacle**; **Temple, Jerusalem**.)

judgement

A basic conviction of the Bible that the will of God must and will prevail, and be seen to prevail. The means by which this revelation and fulfilment of his purposes comes will inevitably involve judgement in some form or other, since whatever contradicts his plans finds itself obliterated by the unstoppable force of his will. Thus, by a strange paradox, judgement is part of the process of salvation, in that it is the means by which all who would dare to stand over against the love and grace of God, as declared in his Law and embodied in Jesus of Nazareth, find themselves overwhelmed by the sheer power of that love. This notion of judgement is more profound and far-reaching than any simplistic concept of a 'great assize' in the sky, where the books are brought out and a tally taken. Rather, judgement is the necessity implied by the truth of a God whose very nature requires that he prevails. (See also **salvation**.)

Judgement Day

The Bible's way of drawing everyone's attention to the belief that, when it is time to draw this era to a close, God will insist on his right to have the last word, and to see the fulfilment of his dream for all creation. The idea is a dramatic way of indicating that this is a matter of crucial seriousness, especially for those who would persist in resistance to the loving invitation of God, and the offer he holds out of eternal life. (See also **judgement**.)

Juggernaut

A Hindu God equated with Vishnu. His temple is situated at Puri in East India, and is famous for its Annual Festival. The devotees of Juggernaut were prepared to sacrifice themselves before their God, so gripped were they by fanatical zeal. The name has, as a consequence, come to be associated with any massive force which overwhelms and crushes anything that gets in its way. It is in this sense that the term is now commonly applied to multi-wheeled lorries considered to be an environmental threat on modern roads. (See also **Vishnu**.)

justification

A technical term much used by St Paul to speak of the reality of those who have been at a distance from God being put into a right relationship with him through the work of Jesus Christ. Because of human sin, the openness and fellowship that ought to exist between God the Father and his loved children has disappeared, and instead there is fear, distance, and hiding. God, unwilling to allow that separation to persist, takes action in the person of Jesus, and by his life of obedience, sacrificial death, and victorious resurrection, he brings the separated parties together. Individuals are invited to enter into this renewed relationship, something hitherto impossible because of sin and rebellion. While this important doctrine does not mean that those enjoying the benefits of God's action somehow become perfect it does mean that, as far as God is concerned, what was wrong has been put right, and fellowship and communion can be enjoyed. In all of this, God is the agent of healing, and people the recipients of God's love and grace. (See also **salvation**; **sin**.)

K

Kaddish /'kædɪʃ/

An ancient Jewish prayer, largely in Aramaic, used to mark the end of public worship. Serving in Judaism much as the Lord's Prayer does in Christianity, it offers praise to God, and looks for the coming Kingdom of God. It is usually recited facing Jerusalem. (See also **Judaism**.)

Kali /'kɑːli/

The Hindu Goddess of destruction, who has another role as the great Mother, who gives life to all things. The consort of Shiva, she holds a very significant place among the deities of Hinduism. (See also **Shiva**.)

Kama

The Hindu God of love, also associated with one of the four ends of life in Hindu tradition, in which the pursuit of love or pleasure is seen as a legitimate goal (which ought, however, to be influenced and controlled by considerations of Dharma). The word has come to wider familiarity through the Indian book the *Kamasutra*, with its suggestions for deepening the sensual experience of love. (See also **Dharma**; **Hinduism**.)

karma

The principle that a person's present actions have long-term consequences, meriting reward or punishment. It is a vital ingredient in Indian philosophy and culture, representing a logic of cause and effect, whereby the sum of an individual's actions are carried forward with them from one incarnation to the next, creating either an improvement in their conditions or a deterioration. Such a philosophy has widespread social implications, the poor being presumed to be those people who in a previous life had lived badly, storing up for themselves their present-day predicament, while the powerful and wealthy are credited with good fortune on the basis of their previous good behaviour. (See also **Buddhism**.)

kerygma /kɛˈrɪgmə/

Originally, a priestly or prophetic utterance; from the Greek meaning 'that which is announced'. In New Testament study, it is more generally applied to the Apostles' Declaration of the Christian message of the saving effectiveness of Jesus's death and resurrection, so that Jesus becomes not just the one who proclaims salvation, but is himself the content of that good news. The notion has come to be understood in Biblical scholarship as the core message of the Church, declared in the New Testament. (See also **New Testament**.)

Kiddush /ˈkɪdəʃ/

An important prayer in Jewish tradition, spoken over a cup of wine by the head of the family in the home at the beginning of a meal on the Sabbath, or on a special festival day. Occasionally, it is used in worship in the synagogue to consecrate the Sabbath or a festival. It is also traditionally recited over a drink or bread before the first meal on the morning following such special events. (See also **Judaism**.)

Kingdom of God

The ultimate rule of God over all creation. In its New Testament use, the phrase serves to describe the sovereignty of God within the lives and experience of men and women. Christ announces the crucial importance of God's rule in the hearts of men and women, and urges an eager acceptance of that rule. For the Gospel writers, the Kingdom of God is no abstract idea, but is embodied in the person of Christ. To opt for the Kingdom of God is to choose Jesus Christ, and receive his lordship. Thus, the Kingdom of God is present in Jesus, and becomes a reality in the minds and wills of those who commit themselves to him. (See also **Christianity**; **God**.)

Kingdom of Heaven

An equivalent notion to the Kingdom of God – gospel-writer Matthew's way of expressing its reality and meaning for devout Jews, who would never utter the name of God. Thus, indirectly, Matthew makes his point for the kingdom, while being sensitive to the delicate conscience of the orthodox Jew to whom his Gospel is clearly directed. (See also **Kingdom of God**.)

Koran

The Holy Book of Islam, sacred to all Muslims. It is believed to be the exact and precise Word of God, written in heaven, and revealed bit by bit to the Prophet Mohammed as God's direct message for all humanity. The actual words themselves are sacred, and the Koran can only truly be read in the original Arabic, as delivered to Mohammed by the Angel Gabriel. (See also **Islam**.)

kosher

Said of food prepared according to Jewish law. The Jewish law is very specific about how food should be prepared, and what food is permitted. For Orthodox Jews only certain animals, which must be slaughtered in a particular way according to Jewish ritual, are allowed to be eaten. (See also **Judaism**.)

Krishna

A great hero and teacher in India, in Hindu tradition believed to be the incarnation in human form of the deity Vishnu. The great Indian epic, the Mahabharata, describes his youth and his love affairs, and these amorous connections are interpreted as symbolic of the relationship between the devotee of Krishna and his God. The high point of Krishna's story is when, disguised as a charioteer, in a dialogue with Arjuna just prior to doing battle, he delivers the great moral teachings of the Bhagavadgita. (See also **Hinduism**; **Vishnu**.)

L

Lamaism

The religion of Tibet, whose roots lie in Mahayana Buddhism. Buddhism reached Tibet in the 7th century, where it met opposition from the indigenous religion, Bon. However, in the next century, an Indian missionary, Padmasambhava, blended elements of both religions, and Lamaism emerged. A reformer of the late 14th century, Tsong Kha Pa, founded a school of thought known as the Gelu, its leader acquiring the title of the Dalai Lama, and eventually taking the mantle of spiritual as well as temporal ruler of Tibet. When the ruling Dalai Lama dies, the search goes on to find a child who is believed to be his reincarnation. (See also **Buddhism**; **Dalai Lama**.)

lamb

An animal frequently referred to in the Old Testament as being used in the sacrificial system of Judaism. Traditionally it was a lamb that was killed at Passover, while many of the regular sacrifices at the Tabernacle were lambs. Being a society at first largely based on the economics of sheep-farming, it is easy to see why, in Hebrew culture, the readily accessible lamb should be selected to illustrate the significance of sacrificial ritual. (See also **blood**; **Lamb of God**; **sacrifice**; **shepherd**.)

Lamb of God

A name given by John the Baptist to Jesus: 'Behold the Lamb of God'. Christ is so designated since by his sacrificial death he will be the one whose blood will 'cover' the sins of the whole world, making things right between mankind and God. He does this in a way far superior to the nature of the sacrifice of lambs in the Old Testament: while their sacrifice could hint at such a salvation, only Jesus could realize that salvation. The image of the Passover lamb lies in the background of events surrounding the Last Supper, and the Lamb of God symbol has continued to be an enduring feature of Christian art. (See also **blood**; **Christianity**; **lamb**.)

Last Supper

The final meal shared by Jesus with his disciples – an event which came to have a profound place in the life of the Church; also known in the early church as the *Lord's Supper*. Jesus shared the meal, perhaps the Passover celebration, with his intimate band of followers, inviting them to interpret the simple act of breaking bread and sharing a cup of wine in a spiritual way which set out the reality and meaning of his own death. He broke bread, urging that this should speak to them of his body which out of love would be broken for them, and he poured out wine to direct them to the significance of his sacrificial death. He then instructed them to continue recreating or recalling that meal and its significance as part of their ongoing experience of discipleship, and this has taken place in the sacrament of Holy Communion. In the fellowship of the meal, the sharing of a common loaf and cup symbolize the underlying unity of the church, despite its many divisions, and look forward to a time of future celebration with all of God's people in the 'great feast' of heaven. Thus, in spite of continued controversy over its precise significance – in particular, whether the bread and wine become by a miracle more than they appear to be, or whether the meal is a simple memorial or re-enactment with saving power – the sense of a past event, a present experience, and a future hope are all retained as key ingredients of an event which is central to the ongoing worship of the Church. (See also **Eucharist**; **Passover**.)

Latter-Day Saints

See **Mormons**

laver /'leɪvə/

An important item of ecclesiastical furniture found in the Jewish Temple in Jerusalem; a large bowl, made either of copper or bronze, used by the priests to prepare themselves for their sacred tasks within the worship of Israel. Sometimes as many as ten lavers were available in the Temple to wash the animals that were to be used in sacrifice.

Law, the

A notion of central significance in the development of a religious code of practice which came to shape and dominate the religion of Israel; also called the *Mosaic Law*. From earliest days, the Ten Commandments of God placed obligations on Israel, the initial spareness of the Mosaic Law being overtaken with additions and clarifications until codified laws governing religious and social life became a distinctive feature of the culture. Unlike other codes of law and conduct found in ancient societies around the time of the Old Testament, the Israelite Law was seen as a reflection of the nature of God, who had chosen, in love, to reveal his will in a particular way to Israel – and this clearly gave to the Law a uniqueness which elevated it to a central place in Jewish thought. For the New Testament, the Law was seen always as a partial expression of God's character, valid as an indicator of humanity's true situation, but always in danger of becoming an end in itself, with mankind enslaved to its demand. The new emphasis is that God's law has been fulfilled and displaced by the law of love established by Christ. And the threat implicit in the failure to conform in every way to the demand of the Law has been removed by the free, loving gift of salvation which is the achievement of Christ. (See also **Israel**; **Judaism**.)

laying on of hands

In ancient times, a way of handing on power or strength to another person. The act could also symbolize a passing over of responsibility, such as when the priest laid his hands on the scapegoat, passing on to it the sins of the people, in order that these sins may be carried off into the oblivion of the wilderness. It became, in New Testament practice, a sign of blessing, an act of healing, or a sign of commissioning an individual for a particular role or responsibility within the life of the Church. In later years, the laying on of hands came to be associated with the Church's act of confirmation and at the ordination of clergy. In the Presbyterian system elders also are ordained by the laying on of hands. In all of this a strong visual image is presented, and God is called upon, in the prayers that accompany this act, to be himself the guarantor of blessing, power, or authority. (See also **confirmation**.)

Lent

In the Christian Church, the weeks before Easter, observed as a period of prayer, penance and abstinence in commemoration of Christ's 40-day fast in the wilderness (Matthew 4.2). In the Western Churches, Lent begins on Ash Wednesday: in the Eastern Churches, it begins eight weeks before Easter. (See also **Ash Wednesday**; **Easter**; **fasting**.)

leprosy

In the Bible, a general term for a variety of disfiguring, debilitating, and deadly skin diseases prevalent in the ancient Near East. It was seen both as a threat to the fabric of community life, and as a symbol of uncleanness, requiring rigid separation from the community and ritual satisfaction, before a cure could be accepted and a return to the community permitted. (See also **cleanliness**.)

Levites

A tribe of the people of Israel who came to develop a particular role within the life of the community, serving as priests within the cultic life of Judaism. At one stage in their evolving role, all priests were Levites, though not all Levites were priests. After the exile, the Levites evolved into a secondary order of assistants to the newly-formed priestly elite, having a subordinate status to them. The first line of importance was reserved in the purified cult for those who could trace their ancestry right back to Aaron himself, the first great priest of Israel. (See also **High Priest**; **Judaism**; **priest**.)

liberation theology

A style of theology emanating from Latin America in the 1960s, which has achieved a considerable degree of popularity within many third-world countries. It is based on the conviction that the purpose of Christianity is not simply to do with some future glory, where all will be well, but should deal with the wrongs and injustices of this world here and now. Using the tool of a Marxist analysis of the structures and power bases within society, it emphasizes the crucial role of the Church in taking a message of hope to the poor and oppressed, and seeing a central theme of the Gospel to be a challenge to the powerful, in the name of the underdog and the marginalized. The approach has met opposition both from fundamentalists, who see the focus of the Gospel to be primarily about belief in certain theological statements, and from secular powers, who are the focus of its incisive social challenge. (See also **theology**.)

limbo

In medieval theology, a home for souls excluded from heaven because they have not received Christian baptism. It was a state or abode with a wide-ranging constituency, which included such diverse individuals as unbaptized infants and Old Testament Prophets. Not a place of punishment, it was the domain of the forgotten, a kind of half-way house between heaven and hell. (See also **heaven**; **hell**.)

lingam /'lɪŋgəm/

A phallic-shaped symbolic representation of the Hindu God, Shiva. It had a female equivalent in the **yoni**, which took the shape of the female sexual organs. (See also **Shiva**.)

litany

A style of prayer often used in public worship within the Christian Church. It is a dialogue of communal prayer in which supplications or invocations are made by the leader, to which the congregation responds with prayers of a fixed form. It is a form of prayer which offers the benefit of considerable congregational involvement in a direct way. (See also **prayer**.)

Liturgical Movement

A determined movement for reform within the worship of the Christian Church. It was motivated by a desire to increase the actual participation of the laity in shaping and developing forms of worship, so that these forms might more effectively relate to the needs of congregations. Begun in the 19th century within the Roman Catholic Church, it grew in influence to embrace other denominations, largely through the role of the World Council of Churches and the wide thrust of the ecumenical movement. (See also **liturgy**.)

liturgy

A term whose original Greek sense was 'duty' or 'service', later 'duty to worship God', and now the form of the service expressing this worship. The notion thus includes the music, words, symbols and order of ritual used to enhance worship and keep it alive for those participating in it. The basic ingredients of Christian liturgy have been borrowed from Jewish ritual, but there is no set pattern of liturgy within Christianity, as different ways of thinking, cultural differences, and so on have shaped the development of a rich variety of liturgical styles. (See also **Liturgical Movement**; **worship**.)

Logos

See **Word**

Lord's Prayer

A prayer taught by Jesus to his disciples when they asked him to 'teach them to pray', often called the 'Our Father' or 'Pater Noster' (Latin) from its opening words. Learned by millions as their first and most important Christian prayer, the Lord's Prayer has crossed cultural barriers, and is commonly used in circumstances of extreme crisis. The original prayer was supplemented with a short text of praise (or doxology: 'for thine is the kingdom . . . ') to enable the prayer to be used in public worship, as well as private devotion. However, this is not used routinely by all denominations (eg by Roman Catholics). (See also **prayer**.)

Lord's Supper

See **Last Supper**

lots, casting of

A method used in the Old Testament to discover the will of God or to reach a decision of some kind; for example, the Promised Land was divided between the twelve tribes of Israel on the basis of casting lots. The practice was carried over into the New Testament, where the soldiers gambled for the cloak of Jesus, and it was the way in which a successor to the traitor Judas was decided upon. (See also **Urim and Thummim**.)

Lucifer

A name applied to Satan, or the Devil, from around the 3rd century AD. Originally it meant simply the 'bringer of light', and seems to refer simply to the King of Babylon. The name is used in two passages in the New Testament, Luke 10.18 and Revelation 9. 1–11, and it is in the light of these mentions that it became associated with the Devil. (See also **Satan**.)

Lutheranism

Churches which have their beginnings in the Reformation inaugurated by Martin Luther (1483–1546) and the doctrines he propounded. They originally sprang up throughout Germany and Scandinavia, and later as a result of persecution spread to the USA. The work of missionaries took Lutheranism to Africa and Asia. The key doctrines are summed up in the Augsburg Confession (1530), the Apology (1531), Luther's two catechisms, and the Formula of Concord (1577). These are the rediscovery of the New Testament doctrine of salvation by faith alone, the recovery of the centrality of the Scriptures, and the affirmation of the priesthood of all believers. Luther also allowed three sacraments – baptism, Eucharist, and penance. In 1947 the Lutheran World Federation was founded – a free association of Lutheran churches which remains the largest confederation of Protestants. (See also **Reformation**.)

M

Magi /ˈmeɪdʒaɪ/

In the New Testament, those who came seeking the significance of the new star and who found themselves written in to the drama of the birth of Christ. The word is from Greek, meaning 'magicians', and is loosely translated as 'astrologers' or 'wise men'. Their discovery of the child, some days after his birth, is known in the Church calendar as *epiphany* – seen as a moment of universal revelation when the Gentiles are invited to acknowledge the saviour who is born in Bethlehem.

magnify

In religion, to praise, honour, or glorify – a notion which expresses the desire to give proper place to God. The notion has given rise to one of the classic hymns of praise in the New Testament, the *Magnificat*, which expresses Mary's joyful celebration of the greatness of God, after learning of her blessedness in being chosen as the mother of God's Saviour.

Maharishi

In Hindu thought, a spiritual leader or Guru, gifted with a special understanding and authority to teach a way of life and instruct in wisdom. Perhaps the best-known example for people in the West is the Maharishi Mahesh Yogi, whose cult of Transcendental Meditation has enjoyed widespread publicity both in the media and through the enthusiasm of his devotees. (See also **Guru**; **Hinduism**.)

Mahayana

The style of Buddhism most commonly found in China, Tibet, Korea, Japan, and Nepal. With its origins in 1st–century Buddhism, as practised in North India, it finds expression in popular religious activity and enthusiasm as laid out in the teaching of the Bodhisattvas. (See also **Bodhisattva**; **Buddhism**.)

Mahdi

One who appears within the community of Sunni Muslims to encourage and inspire people to renewed enthusiasm. An integral part of Sunni Muslim theology is the expectation that, prior to the Last Day, a Mahdi will appear on earth who will establish an earthly kingdom of peace and justice. For Shi'ite Muslims the Mahdi is identified as the hidden Imam who will reappear to bring in his reign of truth and justice. However, this expectation has resulted in a whole series of Islamic leaders claiming to be the true Mahdi, and taking upon themselves the authority associated with the role. (See also **Imam**; **Islam**.)

mandala /'mɑ:ndələ/

Symbolic designs found chiefly in Hindu and Buddhist religious art, understood to represent the structures and essence of the universe, or other aspects of these religions. The mandala are aids to devotion and meditation, acting as focal points to concentrate the mind and inspire it to profound reflection on truth.

Mandeans or Mandaeans

A remnant of Gnostic thought, found in Iran and Iraq, who adhere to the philosophy that a redeemer, Manda D'Hayye, will liberate the human soul from the constraints of a material world that is evil and restrictive. The name means 'knowledge of life'. (See also **Gnosticism**.)

Manicheeism

An ancient religious sect, founded in Persia in AD 240 by a prophet Manes, or Mani, who emphasized in his teaching the contrast between the worlds of darkness and light. He saw the material world as an assault on the realm of light by the powers of darkness, and his idea of the meaning of the religious life was to liberate the light trapped in the material element of the universe. Great religious leaders such as Buddha, Jesus, and Manes himself have come into the world, it was argued, to aid in the process of releasing the light. To break free of the darkness of matter requires a strict, ascetic lifestyle. Manes was executed by the Zoroastrians – but in spite of (or perhaps because of) this,

Manicheeism remained an influential strand of thought within the Christian tradition until as late as the 10th century. (See also **Zoroastrianism**.)

Manitou

The mysterious power of nature held to pervade the natural world, recognized by the Algonquin Indians of North America. The name was used for the whole realm of the supernatural, and for any expression of it in nature, including the physical world as well as humans and animals.

mantra

In Hinduism and Buddhism the repetitive chant of a particular phrase, word, or syllable as part of meditation and prayer, serving to focus the mind and enabling spiritual strength to be developed. A spiritual director will give each disciple an individual mantra, as a sign of initiation, and this will be an important tool in the development of the discipline of devotion. (See also **Buddhism**; **Hinduism**; **meditation**; **om**.)

Maronite Church

A small Christian community which began in the 7th century in Syria, looking to St Maro (died AD 407) as its founding father. Although it deviated from orthodox theology by adopting the Monothelite view (that Christ had two natures but only one will) and although it was condemned for that emphasis in AD 680, the Maronites survived chiefly in Syria, and since AD 1182 the Maronite Church has been recognized to be in communion with the Roman Catholic Church.

Masoretes /ˈmæsəriːts/

Jewish scholars who played a significant part in preserving ancient traditions connected with the Hebrew Bible, and in particular for devising a system of linguistic aids to enable the pronunciation of ancient Hebrew to be expressed in written texts. Thus it is possible to know how the language of ancient texts actually sounded in the original setting. The version they produced in the 9th and 10th centuries AD came to be called the Masoretic Text, and this has become the basis for the text of the Hebrew Bible today. (See also **Bible**.)

Mass

In the Roman Catholic and Anglo-Catholic Churches, the service of liturgical worship which has as its focus the celebration of the Eucharist. It is the central feature of Roman Catholic worship, performing a variety of liturgical roles – such as a Requiem Mass for the dead, a Nuptial Mass at a wedding – as well as serving as the fundamental experience of the peoples' regular religious life. The interpretation of the significance of the bread and wine during the Mass stems from the Council of Trent, where the doctrine of transubstantiation was developed to clarify the meaning of the elements within the Sacrament, taking them in some way to 'become' the body and blood of Jesus. The Mass is accordingly seen as a divine, propitiating sacrifice – a view clearly different from that of the churches in the Reformed tradition. (See also **Eucharist**; **liturgy**; **Missal**; **Requiem**; **transubstantiation**.)

mediator

Someone who intervenes between parties in order to reconcile them. The notion presupposes a problem which, for the Bible, is the loss through human sin of the relationship of joyful communion that *should* exist between mankind and God. Various forms of mediation have been used. Great figures in Israel's history, with special access to God, interceded for the nation to varying degrees of effectiveness. In the absence of such spiritual giants, the system of sacrifices, and the priests who carried them out, helped to build bridges of healing and restoration, though the New Testament saw these as inadequate methods of healing the breach. The perfect mediator, according to the New Testament, was Christ, who was able to intercede in a unique way through the perfection of his sacrifice, and the completeness of his obedience. (See also **sacrifice**; **sin**.)

meditation

The practice of concentrated thought and devoted reflection on some aspect of religious belief or conviction. A common feature in many religions, it has a variety of benefits for the practitioner. A deepened grasp of meaning follows from such continuous and disciplined thought, a grasp of truth that simply would not occur, were time and commitment not given to the practice of meditation. The final goal of such meditation can be a sense of losing oneself in the divine, being so absorbed with the concentration upon God that the individual will is absorbed momentarily by that divine will, giving a glorious state of blessedness and peace. Because meditation is a demanding activity of the mind, it can be helped by adopting particular ways of sitting, finding contexts where meditation is uninterrupted, and by physical aids to devotion such as breathing, repetitive chanting, complete silence, or contemplation of a religious icon. (See also **mantra**; **Transcendental Meditation**; **yoga**.)

Mennonites

A Christian community, largely based in the USA, but with roots in the Anabaptist movement of the 16th century. Its name derives from one of their original founders, Menno Simons (1496–1559). The main element in their system of belief can be found in the Confession of Dordrecht (1632). Their creed required baptism only on confession of faith, the adoption of pacifism, the utter refusal to take on civic responsibility, and a strict adherence to the teaching of the New Testament. (See also **Anabaptists**; **Brethren in Christ**.)

menorah /mɪˈnɔːrə/

The seven-branched candelabrum, an ancient symbol of Judaism. It was initially part of the furnishings of the Tabernacle in the wilderness, and later of the Temple at Jerusalem. The symbol was adopted as the official symbol of the state of Israel in 1948. (See also **Tabernacle**.)

mercy seat

A platform of gold, measuring $2 \frac{1}{2}$ x $1 \frac{1}{2}$ cubits, on top of the Ark of the Covenant. It was considered to be the throne of God where, in the mystery of his living presence, he addressed his people through the mediation of the High Priest. On the occasion of the Day of Atonement, as an action to deal with the sins of the nation, the High Priest would sprinkle sacrificial blood on the mercy seat. (See also **Ark of the Covenant**.)

Messiah

The Hebrew word for Christ, which means the 'anointed one' – someone designated, by the pouring of sacred oil, as having a particular function within the life of the people. Kings were so anointed, so the term carries an implication of kingship. It was a traditional conviction among the Jews that in times of crisis God would send someone to rescue his people, and the model for that deliverer was King David, whose reign epitomized the highest dreams of Jewish aspiration. As crisis upon crisis befell the Jews in the centuries prior to the coming of Christ, so this looking for a special leader who would restore Israel to its former majesty grew in fervour, and the idea developed overtones of supernatural power and influence.

The New Testament acknowledges the contemporary enthusiasm among an oppressed people for the coming of such a mighty warrior king, but it equally makes clear Jesus' refusal to let the distortions that had crept into the idea of the Messiah deflect him from his own role as servant and as one who would suffer. The New Testament writers are very clear in their conviction that Jesus is the Christ, and that the reactions to his presence arose from his refusal to conform to the popular notion of what a Messiah would say or do. (See also **Advent**; **Messianism**.)

Messianism

An expression of Judaism which anticipates a new age of perfection when, with the coming of the Messiah, the ancient Temple will be restored in Jerusalem, and serve as the centre for the Messiah's global rule. In Orthodox Judaism, the emphasis is on the role of the longed-for deliverer sent by God to restore the fortunes of the Jews. Reformed Judaism, on the other hand, interprets the new age in terms of a world socially transformed by the influence of Judaism as a creative force. (See also **Judaism**; **Messiah**; **Zionism**.)

Methodism

A denomination within the Christian Church founded almost accidentally by John Wesley in England in 1779. Originally intended only to be an evangelical pressure group within the Church of England, it became a separate body in 1795. The name comes from Wesley's preoccupation with the need for a disciplined and 'methodical' approach to the Christian life of prayer and Bible-study. He believed that the traditional Church of England, as he experienced it, had become moribund, and needed enlivening by a new evangelical thrust. His theology was mainstream Christian orthodoxy and has resulted in a religious group known for the practicality of their Christianity, the enthusiasm of their commitment, and the energy of their singing. (See also **evangelical**; **Reformation**.)

Michael

An angel at the top end of the heavenly angelic hierarchy. As angels grew to have an increased role in popular religion, Michael began to develop a definable personality and identity. He is seen in the New Testament as an angel who fights with the devil for the corpse of Moses, and as a champion of heaven in the cataclysmic struggle with the dragon, a symbol of evil and deception. (See also **angel**.)

Midras

In Judaism, the explanation and exposition of the contents of Scripture, accumulated during the 1st millennium AD. By investigating the meanings of particular words and cross-referring to other passages of Scripture, the Rabbis sought to bring Scripture to life with relevance and contemporary impact. (See also **Old Testament**.)

Mikado

Since the 10th century in Japan, the name given to the Emperor who in Shinto belief holds an important role in relation to the Gods; the title means 'magnificent door'. A Shinto revival in the 19th century emphasized the sacred place of the Emperor as a descendant of the sun goddess Amaterasu. When in 1868 Shinto was established as the state religion, great adoration of the Emperor followed. Reverence for the imperial role became a cultural reality, and the implication of the Emperor's descent from the sun was that all humanity should worship him. After 1946 Emperor-worship was repudiated by the defeated Emperor in a public broadcast. (See also **Shinto**.)

millenarianism

The belief, held by some Christians, that following the return of Christ to earth to claim his victory, there will be a 1000-year reign of peace, where the saints and the believers will rule the world in justice and righteousness. Revelation 20. 1–7 is the key text. The belief has been a particular preoccupation of certain sects, such as Plymouth Brethren and Adventists, but can be traced back to the very early days of the church. Mainstream Christian thought has not made much of the idea, and the notion has been developed in political and social thought to refer to any religious grouping which anticipates a dramatic change in the world situation as a result of apparent social disintegration or global turmoil. (See also **Adventists**; **Christadelphians**; **Jehovah's Witnesses**; **Plymouth Brethren**.)

minaret

A slender tower with a projecting balcony attached to a mosque, and reaching high above the surrounding buildings; the name originally meant 'place of light'. It serves as the place from which the call to prayer to the Islamic faithful is sounded. Nowadays, minarets are often equipped with a modern public address system so that the faithful from far and wide can be summoned to prayer. (See also **muezzin**.)

minister

An official with spiritual duties in the Christian Church. The original sense was that of 'servant', with the word being used either in a purely secular way, or with reference to a notion of priestly responsibility. It later came to develop, within the history of the Church, the sense of someone with the special role of Christian witness, encouraging others to knowledge and understanding of the faith. Several related interpretations of the word then developed within the various Christian denominations. Among non-episcopal bodies, the term is a general designation for any clergyman. In the Church of England, it refers to the conductor of a service, who may or may not be a priest. In Roman Catholicism, it is increasingly used for a lay person who provides a 'ministry', such as eucharistic ministers and readers. (See also **clergy**; **ministry**.)

ministry

The general term for a particular office or function within a religion. The Old Testament prophets provide an early example of a ministry within the life of Israel. The king in Israel also had a ministry, as a preserver of the Law of Moses and a guardian of the best elements of Israel's culture and religious life. And within the sacrificial cult of Israel's religion, the priests, and in particular the High Priest, had unique religious functions for which they were set apart and honoured. In the New Testament there was a widening of the idea of ministry to include not only the servant role of all Christ's followers, but quite specific callings within the life of the Church. The most important, because the nearest to the source of things, was the ministry of the apostles; but other ministries within the Church also came to be valued, such as deacons, evangelists, leaders, administrators, elders, bishops, superintendents, healers, and workers of miracles. (See also **minister**; **Orders, Holy**; **priest**.)

miracle

A surprising or unexpected event which occurs because of the action of God. Variously, and perhaps more accurately, described as 'signs' or 'wonders', miracles are understood as particular demonstrations of the power of God in our world. The essence of miracles is that they cause a stir because they are beyond comprehension, outside the control of human action. They are understood as being a personal intervention by God in human experience, and are essentially creative, purposeful, and useful, generating praise, thankfulness, and faith. They are believed to happen because people have prayed that they would happen, inviting God and his heavenly power into a situation of crisis or need. Often there is an agent who carries out the miracle in the name of God and this person's credentials are vindicated by the successful miracle. Many of the miracles of Jesus are offered as signs of his lordship and credibility as 'one sent from God'. The effect of the signs is not simply to cause individuals to marvel, but to direct them to God, as the source of salvation. If people see only the miracle, and not the power of God, then the miracle has failed.

Mishnah

In Judaism, an important collection of Rabbinic codes and laws, to be read alongside the specific laws contained within the Jewish Scriptures. The general structure of the Mishnah goes back to Rabbi Akiva and dates from c. 120 AD, but it takes its final form from the editorial work of Rabbi Judah the Pure c. 200 AD. (See also **Old Testament**.)

Missal

The Roman Catholic Church's handbook for worship, giving the specific liturgical forms for use in the celebration of Mass throughout the year. Everything is laid down, including the prayers, the Bible lessons, the form of the ritual, and instructions for special occasions. It is therefore a key tool for clergy and laity in the provision of forms of worship. (See also **Mass**.)

mission

The conviction, put into practice, that the message of the Gospel, of Christ crucified and risen, is to be taken to all the world. It is a crucially important idea within the Christian Church, and arguably the main reason for its existence. The notion derives from the command of Christ in Matthew 28 to 'make disciples'; and mission, the zeal to share the Good News, and draw others within the love of Christ's Church, has been a hallmark of the Church's story. Associated for many years with missionary activity in developing nations, 'mission' is now generally recognized as an ongoing concern of the Church wherever it encounters unbelief. (See also **evangelist**.)

mitre

In the Old Testament, the special headdress worn by the High Priest of Israel. No one is entirely sure what it looked like, but it is thought to have resembled a turban made up of a single piece of linen of the finest quality. This badge of office celebrated the priest's privilege of representing the people before God and the seriousness of that responsibility. The mitre worn by bishops and abbots as part of modern liturgical practice – a high, divided, shield-shaped hat with two bands hanging down at the back – is an echo of this original item of priestly dress. It is intended to symbolize the 'helmet of salvation' referred to in Paul's Letter to the Ephesians, 6. (See also **vestments**.)

Moderator

The person within the Presbyterian Church who acts as chairperson of a Kirk Session, Presbytery, Synod, or General Assembly. His role is to provide a ministry of wise counsel and leadership during the conduct of the business of any of these courts of the Church. (See also **Presbyterianism**.)

Mohammed

See **Islam**

moksha /'moʊkʃə/

Release from bondage to the repeated cycle of rebirth – the chief goal of Hinduism. There is liberation from the force controlling destiny (*karma*) and the attainment of enlightenment (*nirvana*). The moment of release is reached when personal *atman* can be seen to be identical to the universal Brahman, a moment of deep personal realization. (See also **atman**; **Brahman**; **reincarnation**.)

Moloch /'mɒlək/

A Canaanite god from the time of the early settlement of Canaan by the Israelites. An evil and corrupt deity, whose rituals included child sacrifice, Moloch still held enough attraction to the Israelites to seduce them away from the living God. The reforming kings of Israel, who sought to promote the innocence of original forms of Judaism, tried very hard to remove worship of Moloch from the land, but its practices kept reappearing, at least until the time of the Exile.

monasticism

A situation of withdrawal from the experience of normal life into a way of life devoted to prayer, meditation, and the subjecting of the self to the disciplines of spirituality. In both Christianity and Buddhism men (*monks*) and women (*nuns*) have elected for a solitary life of prayer, or a community life, devoted to the quest for a life of purity. The main themes of poverty, and a life of devotion and prayer, emphasize the idea of renunciation of what the world values in order to be free to find a godly life. In Christianity the monastic movement seems to have been begun by Anthony of Egypt in the late 3rd century, and although initially not a clerical order it soon became dominated by the clergy. The Rule of Benedict (c.480–c.547) set the guidelines for monasticism in Western Christianity in the Middle Ages. There are now many different monastic orders, most of which involve vows of poverty, chastity, and obedience. (See also **asceticism**; **Benedictines**; **Carmelites**; **celibacy**; **Cistercians**; **Dominicans**; **Franciscans**; **Ursulines**.)

monotheism

The belief that there is only one God. Emerging from within Judaism, it remains a key element in Jewish, Christian, and Islamic theology. Monotheism is an alternative and opposite view to polytheism, the belief in many gods, and also needs to be distinguished from pantheism, which understands the whole universe to be an expression of God. Some people interpret the Christian Doctrine of the Trinity as a denial of monotheism; but this claim is fiercely resisted within Christianity, which sees itself as a resolutely monotheistic faith. (See also **pantheism**; **polytheism**.)

Montanism /ˈmɒntənɪzm/

An influential movement in 2nd-century Christianity, founded by Montanus of Phrygia with two women (Prisca and Maximilla) whose ecstatic utterances and prophecies of the imminent end of the age attracted the support of churches in Asia Minor. The Catholic Church was opposed to the fringe nature of the Montanist movement, seeing it as a threat to the stability and authority of the institutionalized Church. Though comparatively brief in its existence, Montanism spread its influence surprisingly widely within the early Church's thinking.

monstrance

A liturgical vessel used in the Roman Catholic Church to display the consecrated bread (*host*) used in the Eucharist. It is usually made of silver or gold with a small glass window in its centre.

Moonies

See **Unification Church**

Moral Rearmament

A spiritual movement founded in 1938 by Frank Buchman (1878–1961). Its original purpose was to bring about a deepening of spiritual life, and a more distinctively Christian moral stance among Christians of all denominations. There was an emphasis on divine guidance, on adherence to the principles of honesty, purity, unselfishness, and love, and on public 'sharing' of shortcomings. Inevitably, the movement expanded to include a Christian response to contemporary political and social issues, and after World War II offered an alternative to capitalism and communism.

moral theology

The examination of ethical issues and moral concerns from a Christian perspective. Using the Bible, Christian tradition, and philosophical disciplines, the subject has a wide range, operating on two main levels: (i) it reflects on the foundation of morality, and on such notions as the nature of sin, responsibility, and freedom; and (ii) it studies the social and political dilemmas of contemporary ethics such as abortion, euthanasia and genetic engineering, in order to promote an informed Christian response. (See also **theology**.)

Moravian Brethren

A Protestant sect influenced by Pietism, founded in Bohemia in the 15th century. Scattered by persecution in 1722, the movement spread throughout Europe. Following its establishment in North America in 1734, the USA became the main centre of the Moravian Church today. Its chief characteristics are a quiet spirituality and a non-aggressive gentleness of attitude. (See also **Pietism**.)

Mormons

A religious movement, founded by American religious leader Joseph Smith (1805–44), following a visionary experience in 1830 in Fayette, New York; properly known as the 'Church of Jesus Christ of Latter Day Saints'. Smith's conviction was that he had been led to the Book of Mormon written on sacred golden plates and buried 3000 years previously on a hill near Palmyra, New York. With the help of an angel, and a special pair of sacred spectacles, Smith claimed to have translated the book, which gives an account of an ancient native American people to which Christ himself appeared following his Ascension, and teaches that Christ will found a new Jerusalem in America. Driven by persecution, the Mormons, under the charismatic leadership of Brigham Young (1801–77) moved to Utah, where they established a settlement by the Great Salt Lake.

Mother of God

See **Annunciation**; **Christianity**; **Virgin Birth**

muezzin /muːˈɛzɪn/

In Islam, the official in the mosque whose role is to call the faithful to prayer. A familiar sound in the cities of Islamic countries is the haunting call of the muezzin, echoing over the rooftops, summoning the Muslim population to their religious duty of prayer. (See also **minaret**.)

mullah

A scholar or teacher in Islam, a devout man of religious experience and learning, regarded with respect and influential within the Islamic community. It can also refer to those within Islam who have duties relating to the practice of Islamic Law. (See also **Islam**.)

Muhammad

See **Islam**

myrrh

A fluid obtained from the bark of several trees of East Africa and Arabia, used to make the sacred oils for ceremonies of anointing. Because it was highly scented it was also used for its perfume in cosmetics. It is no accident that myrrh is recorded as one of the gifts of the wise men to the baby Jesus. Since myrrh was used in burial procedures, the symbolism points to his death. (See also **perfumes**.)

mysticism

The pursuit of direct knowledge or experience of the reality of God. Mysticism is an important element in many religions, using prayer, meditation, contemplation, and fasting as channels and disciplines to generate a setting where the life of God may touch against the life of the believer with directness and power. In Christianity, mysticism often demonstrates a particular devotion to the sufferings of Christ. Well-known Christian mystics include St Augustine, St Francis of Assisi, and St Teresa of Avila. This kind of mysticism is not to be confused with one in which the aim is for the individual to be somehow absorbed within the reality of God, as in certain Eastern religions; rather, the desire is to so focus the spirit of the believer upon God that an experience of real spiritual communion can be enjoyed.

N

Nativity

In Christianity, the stories surrounding the birth of Jesus as described in the Gospels of Matthew and Luke. Although the date of the actual birth of Christ is not known, it is generally held to have been around 6 BC. It was not until the 4th or 5th century AD that 25 December became the festival at which the birth of Jesus was celebrated by Christians.

Nazarite

In the Old Testament, men who had specifically consecrated and committed themselves to God; the word derives from a Hebrew root meaning 'dedicated'. They indicated the seriousness of their commitment by refusing wine or liquor of any kind, never cutting their hair, and avoiding anything dead (dead things carrying the implication of ritual uncleanness). One of the most famous Nazarites was Samson – though hardly an orthodox one, judging by his actions in marrying a pagan, having his hair cut, and delving into a dead lion to get some honey. The New Testament record seems to suggest that John the Baptist might well have been one of the 'dedicated' ones.

neighbour

An important Semitic notion, reinterpreted and given universal application by Jesus in his parable of the Good Samaritan. The Law of Moses clearly delineated the obligations of neighbour to neighbour, though the relationship was confined to fellow Israelites to whom certain obligations were owed. Jesus broadens the whole concept to refer to 'whoever needs help'. Anyone, including those against whom one is prejudiced, deserves to be considered as a neighbour, and receive all the help, support, and love that would be given naturally to a neighbour or fellow countryman.

neo-Thomism

See **Thomism**

New Testament

The source book of the Christian Church. It contains a mixture of types of literature, including letters to individuals and to churches purporting to come (and in some cases actually coming) from the pens of apostles, some apocalyptic writing directed to the Church under persecution, and a new kind of writing, the Gospels, written to persuade the unbeliever to faith and to preserve the immediate record of those most closely associated with Jesus and with the beginnings of the faith. The New Testament clearly sees itself as in continuity with the Old Testament, but by way of being a fulfilment of it, speaking about the one to whom the whole Old Testament is pointing – the Messiah. (See also **Apocrypha**; **Bible**; **Canon of Scripture**; **Gospel**; **kerygma**; **Old Testament**.)

Nicene Creed /ˈnaɪsiːn/

A formal statement of the essentials of Christian belief, drafted at the Council of Nicaea in AD 325, and still in regular use today. Used as part of the liturgy of the Eucharist in Orthodox and Roman Catholic Churches, it also has an honoured place in the ritual of many Protestant Churches.

Ninety-five Theses

A list of 95 complaints drawn up by Martin Luther in 1517, highlighting the problems existing within the 16th-century Roman Catholic Church, with its practices of indulgences and clerical corruption, and its emphasis on papal authority. Luther pinned the document on the chapel door of Wittenberg Castle, in an act of defiance which sparked and then fuelled the Protestant Reformation. (See also **Reformation**.)

nirvana

In Buddhism, the attainment of supreme bliss, peace, and perfection. It is the ultimate goal of everything, when all desire has been removed, and the self can be absorbed into the perfection of the Infinite. (See also **Buddhism**.)

Nonconformists

Those Protestants in England and Wales in the 17th century who refused to accept the basic principles of the Church of England, or conform to its practices. It later came to be applied to a whole range of denominations within the Christian Church – such as Baptists, Congregationalists, and Methodists – who resist the assumption underlying the particular place in society and ecclesiastical structures of the Church of England. Indeed, any Christian group which refuses to conform to the particular doctrines or practices of an established church is generally referred to as nonconformist. (See also **Church of England**; **Puritanism**.)

numinous

A feeling for the spiritual that is present in religious experience. It is a sense of awe and wonder, of fascination and fear, in the face of a reality above and beyond our normal experience. It has been described by German theologian Rudolf Otto (1869–1937) as a feeling of the oneness of God drawing near to touch the spirit of man.

nun

See **monasticism**

O

oath

A promise or commitment which calls upon God to bear witness to the genuineness of a vow, freely undertaken; also, an invitation for God to serve as a witness to the veracity of a statement. The Old Testament views oaths with great seriousness, indicating that to go back on an oath is an act of dangerous bad faith. Since swearing an oath has brought the holy power of God into the situation, that power becomes available to punish anyone who goes back on an oath, or commits perjury. (See also **vows**.)

obedience

A central idea in the religion of the Old and New Testaments, expressing the authority of God as creator and Lord, and the relationship of men and women with such a God. Indeed, for the Bible, the problems all begin with an act of disobedience, when Adam and Eve 'fall' at the first hurdle, and disregard God's express instruction about the tree of knowledge of good and evil. Disobedience is seen as a denial of love for God, and a failure, having heard his will, to take that will seriously. When Christ comes, it is precisely his readiness to obey the will of the Father in all things which sets him apart from the rest of humanity, and enables his life to be efficacious for humanity.

occultism

Belief in the action or influence of supernatural powers, and in the attainment of secret knowledge enabling human beings to make contact with them. This contact can be established using a variety of ways, such as magic, sorcery, witchcraft, divination, and certain forms of spiritism. Occultism, because of its emphasis on secrecy and the nature of its ritual, appeals to the darker side of the human quest for the spiritual world, avoiding the way of religious practice as expressed in mainstream religion. Judaism and Christianity have remained, from the earliest of times, highly suspicious of these practices, seeing them as poor substitutes for the hunger for God which they believe to be the way to true spiritual experience. (See also **divination**; **Rosicrucianism**; **witchcraft**.)

Office, Divine

In the Roman Catholic tradition, and in the practice of the pre-Reformation Western Church, the daily spiritual discipline of prayers which priests and others in religious life have to offer every day. The practice, deriving from ancient Jewish tradition, dates from early monasticism. (See also **breviary**.)

oil

See **anointing**

Old Testament

The story of God's commitment to the Jewish people, from their earliest days to a period prior to the coming of Christ. The books tell of God's particular relationship with the people of Israel, who were chosen by him to serve as a focal point of revelation. The Old Testament texts are traditionally described as Law, Prophets, and Writings – a library of various books, representing a whole range of styles and purposes, such as liturgical laws, ancient histories written from a nationalistic and religious perspective, poems and hymns, prophetic writing, and wisdom literature. They are written in Hebrew, with some parts in Aramaic. The work was translated into Greek in the *septuagint*, in order to be accessible to Jews scattered around the world. For Christians, too, the Old Testament remains a book of enduring significance, containing insights into the will of God which have not lost their uniqueness, and all the while pointing – as they believe – to the coming Messiah, identified by the Church as Jesus. The Old Testament is best understood, Christians affirm, when seen through the lens of the Christian Gospel; just as the New Testament comes alive with a new richness when taken in continuity with the Old Testament. (See also **Apocrypha**; **Bible**; **Canon of Scripture**; **Israel**; **New Testament**; **Septuagint**.)

om

A syllable believed by Hindus to have a mystical significance and divine power. It is used at the beginning and ending of Hindu prayer, as a mantra for meditation, and as a way of calling upon God. (See also **mantra**.)

omnipotence

An aspect of the eternal nature of God, expressing his absolute power and freedom to act as he wills. There is no force stronger, and no inhibition can hinder him accomplishing his will.

omnipresence

An aspect of the eternal nature of God expressing the theological view that God is everywhere and in all things, and that spatial notions have no application to him. God is conceived as someone who transcends space and time, yet who is to be found at every place and at every moment, filling all creation with his Spirit.

omniscience

An aspect of the eternal nature of God, expressing his comprehensive and complete knowledge of all things, past, present, and future. Such knowledge raises many questions in religion, not least of which is the question of how the notion of God's foreknowledge can be reconciled with that of human free will. (See also **predestination**.)

one

A term commonly used to summarize the unity, transcendence, and wonder of God. 'The Lord our God is one Lord' (Deuteronomy 6. 4) is the key idea which the Old Testament uses to contrast God with the variety of gods available to the pagans. For a monotheistic religion like Judaism, there is one God and only one; and within the nature of that God is a unity of intention, action, and will. The notion is important, too, in the New Testament, where Christ prays that his Church will be one with him, as he is one with the father. As the characteristic feature of God is oneness, so similar unity is to be a characteristic of the Church.

ontological argument

One of the traditional arguments which attempted to prove the existence of God, originating with St Anselm. It argues that because we can conceive of the existence of an absolute and perfect being, it necessarily follows that such a being must exist. Kant in particular found the argument wholly inadequate. (See also **God**.)

Opus Dei

A Catholic society, founded in 1928, which encourages the exercise of Christian devotion by those engaged with secular society and challenged by the pressures of that society to conform to its values. In some countries, notably Spain, the society has developed a political identity and involvement which has given it a controversial standing. Its methods of acquiring members, as well as the disciplined nature of its spiritual regime, have likewise on occasion been sources of controversy.

oracle

A divinely inspired indication of the nature of future events, delivered by a suitably inspired individual, or discovered in a sacred location (such as Delphi, in Greece). The Bible describes oracles occurring in symbolic as well as verbal expressions, or sometimes even through the simple expedient of casting lots. Oracles differ from plain prophecies in Old Testament thought because a prophecy would usually be given without prior seeking by the prophet, whereas the enjoyment of an oracle presupposes a specific request for guidance on a particular matter. (See also **prophecy**.)

Orders, Holy

The grades of ministry within the Orthodox, Roman Catholic, and Anglican Churches. The 'top grade' of ministry comprises the *Major Orders* – ministers, bishops, priests, and deacons; *Minor Orders* include lectors, porters, exorcists, and acolytes. Further distinctions are made between *First Orders*, men fully committed to Christian service; *Second Orders*, women so committed; and *Third Orders*, those connected to one of the mendicant orders, living in a religious community or in the world. (See also **ministry**; **monasticism**; **tertiaries**.)

original sin

An ancient Christian doctrine which interprets the story of the Fall of Man, in the Book of Genesis, as containing the implication that all human beings inherit a human nature which is flawed as a result of being the offspring, however distant, of Adam. Human nature thus carries within it the stain of sin, and from its very conception needs spiritual rebirth and salvation. (See also **Fall, the**; **sin**.)

Orthodox Church

A communion of self-governing churches, acknowledging the honorary primacy of the Patriarch of Constantinople, and adhering to the theology expounded at the seven ecumenical councils from Nicaea 1 in AD 327 to Nicaea 2 in AD 787. They include the churches of Russia, Bulgaria, Cyprus, Georgia, Serbia, Greece, Poland, Rumania, Czechoslovakia, and Albania. Strongly Trinitarian in doctrinal emphasis, episcopal in government, and with a deep liturgical devotion to the sacraments, it recognizes the ecumenical councils as enjoying final authority. (See also **Christianity**; **Trinity**.)

Oxford Movement

A movement initiated in 1833 to rediscover the High Church doctrines of ceremonial which its supporters believed were in danger of being lost to the new liberalism of the Church of England. The movement was inspired by tracts produced by a group of Oxford theologians, including John Keble (1792–1866) and John Henry Newman (1801–90). Its emphasis on a proper understanding of the place of ritual, along with the rejection of certain reforming tendencies, led to Anglo-Catholicism. (See also **Anglo-Catholic**.)

P

pagoda

In Buddhism, a multi-storied sacred tower, with each storey having an upturned, projecting roof of glazed tiles, its original purpose being to act as a repository for holy relics. With its symbolic structure representing the world as encountered by the worshipper, pagodas provide a tranquil setting for meditation, and are an important element in Buddhist religious practice.

Palm Sunday

In Christianity, the Sunday before Easter. It recalls the occasion when Jesus rode on a donkey into Jerusalem as part of a crowd waving date-palm branches – traditionally used as a sign of rejoicing. The implied symbolism of the arrival of a 'king' coming in peace and innocence did not escape the attention of the anxious authorities, who saw in this event a direct challenge from the preacher of Galilee. (See also **Easter**.)

pantheism

The belief that God and the whole universe are one and the same. A feature of both Buddhism and Hinduism, the notion has received many interpretations. It can be taken to mean that since the only reality is the divine then the sensual world of our experience is an illusion. Or it may be taken to mean that, whenever we encounter the world, there we meet God: 'split a tree, and there is God'. (See also **monotheism**.)

parable

A short story or illustration which highlights a spiritual insight. It was a popular form of instruction among Jewish teachers, intended to draw ordinary people into the meaning of a truth. Jesus used parables to greatest effect as a way of making concrete the abstract truths of his gospel of the Kingdom of God. Although sometimes mistakenly interpreted as allegories, so that every little detail of the story is analysed to see what particular meaning it might have, parables are intended usually to make only one telling point, and the challenge is to find that single pinpoint of truth and respond to it.

Paradise

A place where the souls of the righteous will settle and find happiness; the word has a Persian origin, meaning 'pleasant garden' or 'restful parkland'. For Jesus addressing the thief on the cross ('today you will be with me in Paradise'), it expresses his conviction about the continued existence of the soul after the experience of death. Paul uses the idea to indicate one of the seven levels of heaven believed by Jews to exist, while in the Book of Revelation the idea of Paradise is that of a return to the innocence and perfection of the Garden of Eden. (See also **heaven**.)

parousia /pæˈruːzɪə/

The Christian belief in the second coming of Christ, when God will judge the world and raise the dead in a general resurrection; the word has a Greek origin, meaning 'arrival'. Some Christians continue to look for the fulfilment of the event, predicted in the Gospels and awaited by Paul and the early Church, which will be accompanied by signs and portents indicating its imminence.

Parseeism or Parsiism

A religion which owes its allegiance to the way of Ahira Mazda, the ancient God of the Zoroastrian religion. Parsees live in the area of India around Bombay, and are devoted to a strict rule of life as laid down by Mazda, Lord Wisdom. (See also **Zoroastrianism**.)

Passion

In Christianity, the last days of the life of Christ, and the suffering and death he endured. While the word is only used in this way once in the New Testament (Acts 1. 3), the idea has persisted in Christian thought and literature as a way of gathering up the sense of a growing tempo of threat, danger, and anguish in the final hours of Jesus's life. Passion Sunday is the Sunday before Palm Sunday in the Christian liturgical calendar.

Passover

A meal held annually in April to recall the last night of the Israelites in Egypt prior to their escape in the event known as the Exodus. In an echo of the events of that night, a lamb was killed and the doorposts and lintel of the house sprinkled with its blood, a sign to warn the 'angel of death' to pass over the homes of the Israelites, sparing the Hebrew first-born, while those in Egypt died in the final assault of God's power upon the hardened heart of Pharaoh. There are resonances of the Passover meal in the Last Supper shared by Jesus with his disciples (Mark 14. 12), though it cannot be stated with certainty that this was in fact the Passover meal. (See also **Festival**; **Judaism**; **Last Supper**.)

pastor

A term expressing the role of shepherd within the flock of God, used of leaders and ministers within a congregation. The idea of caring for the people has been a consistent feature of church life since New Testament times (though the actual word appears in the New Testament only once). The role is an echo of Christ's place in the church as the 'Good Shepherd' who cares for his flock.

paten /'pætən/

In Christianity, the silver or gold plate on which the sacred bread used in the celebration of the Eucharist is placed. (See also **Eucharist**.)

Pater Noster

See **Lord's Prayer**

Patriarch

Originally, simply the head of a family or tribe, but in Biblical literature specifically applied to the ten great ancestors of humanity prior to the Great Flood, or more generally to the founding fathers of the twelve tribes of Israel – Abraham, Isaac and Jacob. Since the 6th century the term has been applied as an ecclesiastical title for the bishops of five key centres of the early Church – Alexandria, Antioch, Constantinople, Jerusalem, and Rome. (See also **Israel**; **Tribes of Israel**.)

Pelagianism

A heresy of the 5th century, based on the teachings of a British monk, Pelagius, who took a more generous view of the capacity of human nature to participate in the process of salvation than that taken by orthodox theology. Pelagianism argued that human beings could, using their own natural attributes, contribute to the work of salvation, rather than as forgiven sinners simply receive the salvation of God as his gracious gift. It is as if God's work in bringing salvation required, to be effective, the good judgement of right-thinking men and women. Pelagius' rejection of the doctrine of original sin led to an inevitable clash with the Church, and he was condemned as a heretic at the Council of Ephesus in AD 431. (See also **salvation**.)

penance

In Roman Catholic theology, true sorrow for sin, which includes a turning towards God, and a turning away from sinful paths, in order to receive healing and forgiveness. It involves accepting the role of the Church as a disciplining force which will give opportunities for repentance through prayer, confession, fasting, and good works. (See also **absolution**; **confession**; **reconciliation**.)

Pentateuch /'pɛntətjuːk/

The first five books of the Bible, known as 'the Law' to the Jews, and considered to have been the works of Moses; the word is from the Greek for 'five books'. It is now thought unlikely that all of the books are in fact the work of Moses, though some of the material clearly comes from Moses's time. Scholarship today discerns at least four different sources which go to make up the books, and the unknown authors or editors of these four sources have been designated J, E, P, and D on the basis of stylistic differences. Very early on in Jewish religious life the authority of the Pentateuch as canonical scripture was acknowledged. Indeed, after the division of Israel into Northern and Southern Kingdoms, the Samaritans in the North would recognize only the Pentateuch as authoritative. (See also **Bible**; **Law, the**.)

Pentecost

A feast day held 50 days after the ceremony in which the Jews offered the first sheaf from the harvest, used to mark a successful harvest end. Known by a variety of different names – the Feast of Weeks, the Harvest Feast, or the Day of First Fruits – its purpose was to celebrate the provision of God. For Christians, Pentecost holds the extra significance of being the day of a powerful eruption of the Holy Spirit upon the disciples of the risen and ascended Jesus. Through the gift of tongues they were able to convince a vast crowd of visiting pilgrims of the truth of the Gospel, and so in effect the Church was born. (See also **Holy Spirit**.)

Pentecostalism

A movement for spiritual renewal within the modern Christian Church, looking for a church inspired by the Holy Spirit as it was on the day of Pentecost (Acts 2). Pentecostalism began in Topeka, Kansas, in 1901 and developed an organizational framework soon after. When the established Churches hesitated to welcome this new force, those of a Pentecostalist disposition formed their own 'Pentecostal' churches. The movement has since spread throughout the world, emphasizing an experiential, Bible-based faith with lively spontaneous worship and the evidence of the presence of power of the Holy Spirit with its appropriate gifts. The main features of the movement include speaking in tongues as a sign of a spirit-filled life, the restoration of the gift of prophecy as a regular and accepted element of normal church life, and evidence of the gift of healing. (See also **charismatic movement**; **Holy Spirit**; **Pentecost**; **tongues, speaking in**.)

perdition

A word used to convey the idea of the fearful end awaiting those who persist in rejecting the love of God. It carries all the emphasis of eternal loss, of obliteration from the light and presence of God, and suggests that this will be the fate of the unrepentant sinner who spurns the offer of salvation. Perdition is seen as a self-inflicted consequence rather than the result of actions by a wrathful God, and its reality recognized as one possible way to experience eternity. (See also **hell**.)

perfection

A notion applied in the Old Testament to the quality of the sacrifices brought to the priests, symbolizing the seriousness of sin in the eyes of God, and the reality of God's expectation for purity of life. The New Testament introduces the sense that at last things are complete, with partial knowledge and revelation becoming perfect in Christ. The goal of the Christian life is also to be perfect, in the sense of being so fully committed to God that humanity becomes what it is meant to be, living a life of wholeness and love. Although the notion of perfection has overtones of moral correctness and purity, for the Bible it is principally to do with devotedness to God, and the giving over of self to the service of God's will.

perfumes

Sweet-smelling fragrances used from earliest times for purely cosmetic purposes and in the burial of the dead, and later having a significant part to play in Temple worship in Jerusalem. Sacred perfumes were used as a powerful symbol within the rites of Judaism, being sprinkled on the sacred Covenant Box as a sign of worship and prayer. Perfume is used as a powerful picture in the Bible; 'prayer rising like a sweet odour to God'.

Pharisees

A devout sect of Judaism, significant for almost four centuries before, during, and after the time of Christ. The name originates in the idea of 'separateness' – an indication of the sect's impatience with those whom they reckoned were drifting away from the true rigour of the Mosaic Law. They looked back to Ezra as the hero who had salvaged the purity of Judaism, and saw in him a role-model of piety and exactness in observing the minutiae of the dietary laws and ritual practices which had diminished in importance within the life of the average Jew. Christ found them inflexible, legalistic, and self-righteous, laying too great an emphasis on the letter rather than the spirit of the law. It was in part at least his condemnation of the Pharisees which led to his arrest and execution. (See also **Judaism**.)

Philistines

A people originating in Crete, who sailed to Palestine and settled on the coastal plain c. 1200 BC. The region of Palestine takes its name from these settlers. Absorbed into native Canaanite religious practice they constantly attempted to extend their influence into a wider area, and in so doing came into conflict with the Israelites. They were subdued, according to the Old Testament, during King David's reign. Their role in the Old Testament is as an adversary against whom the Israelites found God's help crucial. They served as a catalyst in the social development of the nation state of Israel, and helped shape its subsequent history. The Israelite view of the Philistines as hostile barbarians has given rise to the modern sense of the word – someone who professes indifference or opposition to aesthetic or intellectual values.

phylacteries

Little boxes fastened by leather straps to either the forehead or arm of a devout Jewish man over the age of thirteen, in which are kept small pieces of parchment on which are written key passages of the Mosaic Law. The origin of the practice lies in Moses's instruction to the children of Israel to treat the Law of God with such seriousness and respect that they are to 'tie them on your arms and wear them on your forehead'. The custom developed in the 2nd century BC as a signal of particular devotion to the law and a literal acceptance of its validity. They are still worn today by orthodox Jews as a badge of devotion. (See also **tefillin**.)

Pietism

A reaction against the Protestant emphasis in the 17th and 19th centuries on doctrine and correct belief, emphasizing a godly life, spiritual discipline in prayer and Bible study, and practical Christian caring. It developed out of Lutheranism as a corrective to rigid dogmatic wrangling, and was an important influence on such diverse religious groups as Moravians, Methodists, Evangelicals, and Plymouth Brethren. (See also **Moravian Brethren**.)

piety

A godliness and seriousness of intent in religious life and practice. It refers to sincerity of belief and the practice of genuineness and loyalty towards God, marked by a practical expression of that love in the humble duties performed towards God and neighbour. It has come to have overtones which are not so attractive – of humbug and display of religious zeal – but this is a departure from its original meaning. The whole weight of Old and New Testaments lies behind the notion that piety is desirable in all those who take God seriously, and is a worthy aim for the spiritual person. It is achieved by the disciplines of prayer, study, worship, and service to others.

pilgrimage

A special journey to a holy place in order to enliven the faith of an individual – an important feature of Islam and Christianity. In Islam it is one of the key pillars of the Muslim religion. In Christianity it is more of an optional activity – a way by which the effort of journeying to a holy site (which need not be a great distance away) intensifies the concentration of mind and spirit to the enrichment of personal faith. The symbolism of pilgrimage has passed into the common imagery of Christian thought, which sees the whole of life as a pilgrimage towards the glory of heaven.

Pillars of Islam

Five foundations on which the Islamic religion is built, shaping the practice of Muslim believers: witness or confession of faith in the one God; prayer, five times a day; alms giving; fasting, especially during Ramadan, the ninth month of the Muslim year; and pilgrimage. These expressions of a practical faith serve as a unifying force within Islam, as well as developing the spiritual life and commitment of the individual Muslim. (See also **Islam**.)

Plymouth Brethren

A small but influential religious sect, founded in Dublin in 1829 by a group of evangelical Christians. In 1832 a meeting was established in Plymouth, hence the name. Plymouth Brethren have a devout belief in the authority of the Bible and try to live their lives and order their congregations according to New Testament practices. They take the Bible literally, and have a millenarian viewpoint, anticipating the imminent coming of Christ. Their hallmarks include an ethical and pious lifestyle, and a genuine desire to evangelize. As early as 1848 they had split into the 'open' Brethren and the 'exclusive' Brethren. (See also **evangelical**; **millenarianism**.)

polytheism

Belief in and worship of more than one god. It is a characteristic of paganism, both as expressed in primitive cultures, and also in the sophisticated cultures of ancient Greece and the Roman Empire. (See also **monotheism**.)

Pope

The title given to the Bishop of Rome who, following in Apostolic succession to St Peter, the first Bishop of Rome, has the role of head of the Roman Catholic Church. The title is also used by the head of the Coptic Church. Elected by a conclave of the College of Cardinals, the Pope draws his authority from a claim to an unbroken connection with Peter. After the churches in the Eastern Roman Empire or Byzantine Church declined in influence, Rome was generally acknowledged to be the focal point of power within the Catholic Church. Now still holding political power as head of the Vatican City in Rome, the Pope enjoys the additional authority of papal infallibility – a claim always held, but officially formalized in the First Vatican Council in 1870. This claim has never been accepted by the Protestant Churches. (See also **cardinal**; **encyclical**; **infallibility**; **Roman Catholicism**.)

prayer

A personal and profound opening of an individual's life in thought and word to the presence and reality of God. At its best, prayer represents a willingness in the worshipper to open the windows of the soul, and let the life and love of God flood into that soul. It often takes the form of simple petitions for God to act on our behalf in some specific way, but can be a far richer and more personally demanding activity, for it includes the baring of the soul in confession of sin to the God who is owed ultimate loyalty, the restoring of the spirit in joyful thanksgiving, and the awakening of the heart to meditation. It is far broader in scope than a mere heavenly 'shopping list' brought by the beleaguered believer. The New Testament recognizes the faltering inadequacy of human prayer, but reassures us that the true inspiration behind praying, and the one who makes it intelligible and true worship, is the Holy Spirit whose power translates our stumbling efforts at prayer into the 'language of heaven'. (See also **Kiddush**; **litany**; **Lord's Prayer**; **Rosary**; **Shema**.)

preaching

Originally, the announcement of news by a herald to a community; thus in the religious context, the proclamation of good news, the Gospel of the Kingdom of God. Only those with a religious message would now be considered to 'preach', for the notion implies a summons by God and a challenge to faith. The authority of the preacher comes from God, whose word provides the rationale and the credentials for the preacher. The message is effective insofar as the power of the Holy Spirit convinces or converts. (See also **evangelist**; **Holy Spirit**.)

predestination

A doctrine devised by theologians to deal with the conundrum that, if God is all-knowing and eternal, he must know that certain people from the time of their birth will choose disobedience instead of faith. The implication of this is that God also knows who will choose the way of eternal life and who will choose the way that leads to eternal damnation. While this is not quite the same as suggesting that individuals are earmarked for destruction, it does raise a problem about a God who would allow people to be born, all the while knowing that the choices they will make will relegate them to eternal punishment. The doctrine of predestination is never fully articulated within the early Church which, while it maintains the view that God knows about everything, insists that individuals have freedom of will and must take responsibility for their actions, and for the consequences which stem from the choices they make. (See also **salvation**.)

Presbyterianism

The conciliar form of Church government of the Reformed Churches, deriving from the 16th-century Reformation led by John Calvin in Geneva and John Knox in Scotland. Government is by courts at local congregational (eg kirk session), regional (presbytery), and national (General Assembly) levels. *Elders* (ordained laymen or laywomen) as well as ministers play a leading part in all courts. Through emigration and missionary activity from Scotland, Ireland, and England, Presbyterianism has spread worldwide. The World Presbyterian Alliance was formed in 1878, to be succeeded in 1970 by the World Alliance of Reformed Churches. (See also **Moderator**; **Reformation**; **Westminster Confession of Faith**.)

presbytery

The Authorized Version's way of referring to all the elders of a congregation, coming together for decision-making. It is a notion which lies behind the form of government of the Presbyterian Church system, with its series of courts or convocations, made up of leaders, elders, and supervisors within congregations in order to deal with matters of policy, discipline, or doctrine. (See also **Church of Scotland**; **Presbyterianism**.)

priest

A person authorized to carry out the sacred rites of a religion, and to act as an intermediary between the people and God; in Anglican, Roman Catholic, and Orthodox churches, a clergyman ranking below a bishop and above a deacon. Even the earliest religions employed the services of a priest to carry out the duties of the ritual, although in their early nomadic life Israelites seemed to have managed without an official order of priests. Instead, the head of the family seems to have been sufficiently qualified to deal with the religious duties of prayer and making sacrifices to God. That changed with the Settlement in Canaan, when the tribe of Levi was chosen to deal with priestly tasks, and the Order of Levitical priests emerged. This practice was later refined until only those who were connected in origin with the family of Aaron were permitted to teach the Law and look after the sacred furniture of Israel's worship. In Israel, the priests were also involved in the teaching of the Law, responsible for codifying and preserving the Hebrew scriptures, and the existence of the Old Testament as we have it is largely due to that endeavour. Gradually, through education and the possession of a key power base, the Temple, the priests developed into an elite within Jewish society, with the High Priest assuming an influential and often political role.

With Christianity, things were radically changed. Jesus was seen as the true High Priest, making a sacrifice, and it is he who intercedes in his risen life on behalf of everyone. In the light of this, the Church enjoys the title and responsibility of being 'a royal priesthood', offering spiritual sacrifices of faith, devotion, and Christian service to God, through the mediation of Jesus. The church engages priests as ministry, the precise content of this idea depending upon the denominational standpoint (in particular the doctrine of Eucharist that is in operation). If the Sacrament of bread and wine is thought of as the 'sacrificing again' of Jesus, then the idea of a priest necessary to make that sacrifice on the altar is a valid one. If the Sacrament, as in the Reformed tradition, is a sacrifice of praise and love from the believers present, the idea of altar or priest no longer applies. (See also **clergy**; **High Priest**; **Levites**.)

primate

The most senior bishop of a given area. The Archbishop of Canterbury enjoys the title of Primate of all England. In the early Church, the name was applied to the Metropolitan of a Province and later to the Patriarch. (See also **bishop**.)

promise

A declaration or pledge that one will act in a certain way. One of the key features of the God of the Bible is that he is a God who, out of love and graciousness, makes promises to his people. He promises Noah no more floods in the sign of the rainbow; he promises the apparently infertile Abraham and Sarah that from them will come the multitudes of Israel; while to David come generous promises of success and successors. Canaan is anticipated by the nomadic Israelites as the Promised Land, and the hope of that assurance sustains the wobbly faith of the wayward people. These promises lie behind the events of Christ, Calvary, Easter, and Pentecost, and the whole emphasis of the New Testament is to express that sense of promises kept and fulfilled in Jesus Christ.

prophecy

The inspired declaration of divine will and purpose. The job of the Old Testament prophet was not primarily to foretell the future, but to declare what the plans of God were, and to summon his people to faith and obedience. It is an unhelpful caricature to think of prophecy as primarily to do with prediction. It was far more likely to be a word of hope, comfort, rebuke, or challenge – commonly a call to abandon the ways of faithlessness, and often made in the middle of national crisis. Prophecy continued in the New Testament, and one of the ministries recognized in the early Church was that of prophets, inspired by the Holy Spirit. (See also **Holy Spirit, oracle**.)

propitiation

The act or process of regaining someone's good will. The idea is used to convey the sense of an angry God being appeased, usually by sacrifice. Its appearance in the Bible is the result of an attempt to translate the idea of 'expiation', and its use gives a shift of meaning which is largely out of tune with Old

Testament thought. While pagans might see their sacrifices in terms of calming down the wrath of their angry deities, the nature of the relationship between the Jews and God was believed to be altogether different, based on the notion of a loving God who did not need to be appeased. The sacrificial system was used for a different purpose – to deal with the reality of sin in a way that did justice to its seriousness. (See also **expiate**; **sacrifice**.)

proselyte /ˈprɒsɪlaɪt/

A new convert, a term originally used for those who chose to attach themselves to the Jewish faith, following circumcision, baptism, and the making of sacrificial offerings. In modern times the word has developed overtones of aggressive evangelism, with missionaries actively searching out unbelievers in order to make conversions. (See also **conversion**; **evangelical**.)

Protestantism

A religious movement begun by Luther in 1516, with his criticisms of the Roman Catholic Church as it then operated, and his arguments against the theological assumptions that lay beneath its practices. Out of this protest developed a brand of Christian faith which laid emphasis on the centrality and authority of the Bible, on justification by faith alone, and on the capacity of all Christians to explore their faith with their own intellect and spiritual insight, rather than be dependent upon the official priesthood for their spiritual understanding. Protestantism soon divided into several distinct beliefs, such as Lutherans, Zwinglians, and Calvinists, and now refers to a wide range of non-Roman Catholic or non-Orthodox denominations. (See also **Lutheranism**; **Reformation**.)

proverbs

A style of writing in which nuggets of wisdom are expressed in short sayings, in down-to-earth language, easily understood and enjoyed by ordinary people. Proverbs were common in Israel, and represent a kind of popular religiosity, devoid of obscure theological elements. People were encouraged to read these sayings and make them their own, as a way of enriching their understanding and bringing great blessing. The practice of creating proverbs is found comparatively early in the history of Israel, with King Solomon a serious patron and practitioner. (See also **wisdom**.)

providence

The notion that God in his wisdom makes provision for the requirements of his people. It is an attempt to address the issue of 'the hand of God' at work in history, and in the rhythms of nature, and in the events of human experience. The notion encounters a difficulty with the violence and tragedies of nature, in a world of famines, earthquakes, holocausts and war. The Bible attempts to deal with the problem by acknowledging the all-powerful and all-knowing nature of God, but at the same time acknowledging the freedom of the human will to disrupt God's plan. God allows the evil consequences of human free will to run their course, thus fulfilling his object, which is to create beings who out of their freedom will turn to him with a love that is real, meaningful, and responsible. Without this responsibility, there would be no humanity.

Psalms

Religious songs used in the worship of the Old Testament. The emphasis of the psalms is the character of God and the rightness of worshipping his majesty and recognizing his authority. Thought for a time to be the exclusive work of David, they are now recognized to have been a form of worship created by a variety of authors, including no doubt David himself. The depth and richness of these sacred poems is such that they have endured over many centuries, expressing the ordinary themes of Israel's religious feelings and experience, but having a universal application for mankind's religious quest, and the tensions of the life of faith. (See also **hymns**.)

punishment

Retribution for an offence. The notion is an inevitable consequence of any religion which takes failures in morality and social responsibility seriously. Punishment is seen in two forms in the Old Testament. First there is the idea of retribution, where the Old Testament addresses a world prone to over-reaction and insists on a restrained balance, that the punishment fit the crime – an eye for an eye, a tooth for a tooth. Also present is the requirement of justice, that restitution be made for the injury and damage done. The Christian view of punishment was to exclude the wrongdoer from the Church community against which the offence had been committed, in the hope that such a debarring from the warmth of fellowship would lead to a change of heart, forgiveness, and restoration. (See also **forgiveness**; **penance**; **sacrifice**; **sin**.)

Pure Land Buddhism

A form of Buddhism believed to have been founded by a Chinese monk Hui Yuan (334–417). It later spread to Japan. Its main characteristic is devotion to the Bodhisattva Amitabha who is believed to rule over a 'pure land'. The aim of those committed to Amitabha is to be reincarnated there, and in so doing to achieve enlightenment. (See also **Buddhism**.)

purgatory

The situation of the dead who suffer for their sins prior to being allowed into heaven. Those still on earth, it is believed, can encourage and help those in purgatory by their faithful prayers. The doctrine of purgatory is particular to Roman Catholic theology and some Orthodox teaching, and has not found any degree of acceptance within the Protestant churches, as it goes against the grain of the idea of salvation by faith alone as a gift of God's grace and by means of the sufferings of Christ.

purification

The ritual of making oneself free of material defilement or imperfections, in order to safeguard the sanctity of religious practices. In the Old Testament, strict rules of ritual purification were laid down, which would protect these practices from contamination by sin. Sex, blood, death, leprosy, and sinful actions were all considered to carry with them the taint of impurity. The methods used to achieve a state of purification were varied, and including searing with fire, ritual washing according to a preordained pattern, and allowing time to pass between sexual activity and worship. (See also **baptism**; **cleanliness**; **washing**.)

Puritanism

A religious movement which had its roots in a reaction against the forms of the Church of England in the 16th and 17th centuries. It is a much-abused concept, often confused in the common mind with attitudes of negative and narrow-minded rejection of what most people would consider normal human enthusiasms. The true spirit of Puritanism is rooted in an eagerness for religious liberty and an early concern for human rights, much more than with narrow moralism. It was this determination which inspired the Puritans in their struggle for nonconformity, in face of significant pressures from king and established Church. The Puritan zeal for religious liberty is found enshrined in the clauses of the American Constitution. (See also **Nonconformists**.)

purple

A colour signifying wealth, and which in the ancient world had associations with royalty. The purple hangings in the Temple were symbols of the majesty of God, and purple has remained a living symbol of authority and glory within the liturgy of the Christian Church. The purple robe placed on Jesus during the humiliations of his trial and execution was a mocking of his claims to kingship. Advent is the season which highlights the use of purple as part of the symbolism of the Christian liturgical calendar.

purpose

A conviction that reality as we encounter it is no mere accident, but part of an ongoing plan of God. A basic assumption of the Bible includes the notion that, in the revelation of the Word of God, and in the demonstrations of his power in the events of history, can be ascertained a divine purpose, expressed through the people of Israel. In the Christian faith, this purpose is held to be expressed finally and supremely in the ministry, death, and resurrection of Christ. According to the New Testament, God's purpose is to bring the whole of existence into a unity of perfection through the power of Jesus. (See also **Providence**.)

pyx

A small metal box used within the Roman Catholic Church to carry the Sacrament to the sick. It can also be a larger box used to reveal the sacred host to worshippers.

Q

'Q'

The name given by Biblical scholars to one of the sources of the New Testament Gospels; derives from German *Quelle* 'source'. It is thought that a number of early source documents were used by the Gospel writers, and Q represents one common thread, thought to have been an early collection of the sayings of Jesus. Mark's Gospel contains much of the material from Q, while Matthew and Luke also include elements of it. (See also **Gospel**.)

Quakers

See **Friends, Society of**

Queen of Heaven

A title ascribed to Mary, the mother of Jesus, in Roman Catholic tradition. Its origin lies in the title of Astarte, or Ishtar, an ancient female mother-earth deity worshipped by the Phoenicians and Assyrians.

Qumran

A settlement at the north-west corner of the Dead Sea, established by an exclusive Jewish sect in the 2nd century BC. They understood themselves to be the remnant of the true Israel, and were anticipating the Kingdom of God. Their lifestyle was simple, and they valued purity and strict adherence to Jewish Law and religious practices. In this, they are thought to have been closely related in character to the sect of the Essenes. During the Jewish uprising against the Romans (AD 66–70) they were wiped out, but their writings, mystical and deeply devoted to the classic scriptures of the Old Testament, were preserved in stone jars until their discovery in 1947, and now form part of what came to be known as the Dead Sea Scrolls. (See also **Dead Sea Scrolls**.)

R

rabbi

A teacher and student of the Jewish Law and its interpretation. Rabbis in the Old Testament were a respected, educated group within the Jewish community, viewed as wise men of integrity and vision. Jesus was addressed with this title on several occasions, as recorded in the Gospel, as was John the Baptist before him. The title and position remains in contemporary Judaism. (See also **Judaism**.)

rainbow

A natural physical phenomenon given religious significance in the story of Noah and the great Flood, when it becomes a sign given by God and his promise never again to destroy the world in this way. The outward manifestation of that undertaking by God was considered to be the sign of the rainbow. (See also **forgiveness**.)

Ramadan

The ninth month of the Muslim year, during which an obligatory fast is laid down by the Koran for all Muslims. During Ramadan, no food or drink is to be taken, other than after dark. The end of Ramadan is marked by a special festival called the Feast of the Breaking of the Fast, or the Little Feast. (See also **fasting**; **Islam**.)

Rapture, The

One interpretation of the New Testament's view of the future, which takes quite literally the idea that living believers will be caught up in the air, and transported 'in the twinkling of an eye' into a state of heavenly bliss. This experience, known as 'The Rapture', will herald the beginning of the end, and the establishment of the Millenial Kingdom. (See also **millenarianism**.)

real presence

The belief that the body and blood of Jesus are actually present in the bread and wine of Communion. Quite what this meant confused and obsessed the Reformers, and a whole spectrum of interpretations continues to exist within the life of the Christian Church. (See also **Eucharist**; **transubstantiation**.)

Rechabites

A religious group with origins in the story of Rechab, whose son encouraged Jehu to slaughter many of the family of King Ahab; the king who had brought the worship of Baal, with all its pagan expressions, into the heart of Israel's life. The Rechabites had an ascetic lifestyle, and disdained anything which smacked of materialism, in particular avoiding alcoholic beverages. As champions of a true loyalty to God they stood in vivid contrast to those Jews who were willing to absorb the corruptions of paganism and to be absorbed by them. Modern-day Rechabites are still totally committed to abstention from alcohol.

reconciliation

The restoration of friendship or harmony. It is a major theme of the Bible, focusing on the separation which has come between God and humanity as a result of persistent sin. In the thought of the Bible the crucial effect of sin is not that it breaks codes of morality, nor that it offends against the laws of God, but that it offends God himself and causes a broken relationship between humanity and God. It is the health, or otherwise, of that relationship which is the key issue. According to the New Testament, reconciliation is achieved through Jesus: 'God was in Christ reconciling the world to himself'. (See also **absolution**; **atonement**; **forgiveness**; **penance**.)

redaction criticism

A type of Biblical scholarship which directs its attention to the authors of the various Bible texts, and the local situation out of which they wrote. The assumption is that this situation would have had a profound influence on the author, inevitably shaping the emphasis chosen and the ideas expressed. This approach considers the historicity of Biblical accounts to be seriously affected by the reasons lying behind their selection. If words attributed to Jesus, for example, are more accurately to be thought of as reflecting what the author of the gospel *thought* about Jesus, then the emphasis shifts radically from 'what might have happened on a given occasion' to 'why the writer believed what he did, and why he tried to express his faith in a particular story or saying of Jesus'. The claim of redaction critics is that what matters is belief and commitment, not factual information and historical accuracy. This is a viewpoint not shared by those who need the feel of solid facts beneath their feet before they can take the step of faith. (See also **Bible**.)

redemption

A notion whose roots lie in the sociology of Israel, where it was accepted practice for individuals to be able to buy back (redeem) property that had once been in the family, but which had through circumstances fallen into someone else's hands. The symbolism of redemption found its way into the idea of God as the Redeemer of his people – the one who redeems them from slavery in Egypt, and later from exile in Babylonia. The issue of who receives the ransom that redeems is not fully considered. It is enough that Israel is out of bondage, and God has brought that liberation to pass. The sacrificial system within Israel also borrows the redemption/ransom theme, applying it to the effectiveness of the sacrifice, which 'covers' the cost of the sin. This same balance exists when the New Testament takes up the theme and applies it with a new finality to the work of Christ. Jesus, the New Testament declares, came to 'give his life as a ransom for many'. An added element is the imagery of the slave-market, with the sinner, the 'slave to sin', doomed to a life without true liberty. In order to redeem or emancipate the sinner, Christ pays the fee of that release in his suffering and death. (See also **sacrifice**; **sin**.)

Reformation

A movement for change and reform in the Christian Church, beginning in the 16th century as a protest against the corruption and power of medieval Roman Catholicism. The Reformation began with Martin Luther, whose challenge to what he saw as abuses and deviations from Biblical teaching and practice triggered an immediate popular response in much of Europe. The inability or unwillingness of the Church to change itself quickly led inevitably to the formation of Protestant churches in several countries. Economic and political opportunism added to that momentum, as powerful nobles saw a chance to make capital from the protest, and to strike at the wealth of the Roman Catholic Church.

Different motivations from those of pure theology drove Henry VIII in the 1530s to make his historic break with Rome, and give the Reformation a strong base in England. John Knox in Scotland in 1560 gave the Scottish Reformation its particular flavour. Once the Reformation was underway, attempts at internal reform, though significant for the Roman Catholic Church, could do nothing to stop the drive for change. (See also **Calvinism**; **Congregationalism**; **Counter-Reformation**; **Lutheranism**; **Methodism**; **Ninety-five Theses**; **Presbyterianism**; **Protestantism**.)

regeneration

A radical change within the life of an individual, prompted and sustained by the Holy Spirit. The notion of being 'born again' has worked its way into the key terminology of Christianity. The concept is introduced by Christ in John's Gospel, where he insists that a prerequisite of 'seeing the Kingdom of God' is that a person be 'born again'. The effect of sin and rebellion is to so disfigure the inner life of a person that they need a whole new start if they are to find the joy of God's kingdom. The new start brings with it different perspectives, and a turning away from the dead old ways of self and sin. Baptism is the indication that the new beginning has come. (See also **baptism**; **charismatic movement**; **Holy Spirit**.)

reincarnation

The rebirth of an individual in another body after death. Many cultures have accepted the idea as part of their religious life. In Hinduism, the precise nature of the rebirth depends upon the previous actions of an earlier life. Those who have done well, will be reborn into an upper echelon of society, but those who have lived badly will endure an evil rebirth in a low caste, or even as an animal. (See also **Hinduism**; **moksha**.)

relics

Material remains, or sacred objects, which have some association with a holy person, such as a saint. They might include the bones of the saints, a piece of the cross, or a scrap of cloth from the tunic of Christ. Relics came to give great status and significance to their possessors. Churches would be built around a relic, and devout pilgrims would come to venerate such precious links with a sacred past. The veneration of relics and the pilgrimages associated with it was a great breeding ground for charlatans, especially in the Middle Ages.

religion

That activity of the human race which seeks to explore the spiritual dimension of existence and to pursue a set of beliefs with which to interpret experience and to live out life in a way coherent with those beliefs. A religion will tend to have a series of doctrines or convictions which express a particular world view, and will involve the individuals loyal to it in a lifestyle which responds to these convictions. It may develop a set of practices and a form of worship through which its adherents can express, enjoy, and communicate their beliefs to others. Religion is concerned with issues of fundamental personal significance, and the pursuit of religion is a clear acknowledgement that such issues exist and deserve attention. Although in a superficial way all the main religions of the world appear to have common features – often a great teacher, a holy book, an ethic, a form of worship, a vision of the future – these similarities are more apparent than real. Religions approach experience in radically different ways and come to very different conclusions. Convenient though it would be to be able to affirm the notion of the common impulse and the equal truth of all religions, it is simply not accurate to do so. (See also **comparative religion**; **cult**; **eschatology**; **God**; **sect**; **worship**.)

remnant

A group of believers who stay loyal to God, regardless of disasters and setbacks. The conviction of the Old Testament is that, however bad things are, God will always ensure that a rump of loyal followers will remain true, preserving the sacred core of the faith of Israel. The New Testament takes up this theme, seeing the Christians who accept Christ as being the true remnant of Israel, now responsible for promoting the truth of Christ in the world. (See also **Israel**.)

repentance

A personal response of regret for sins committed against God. It represents not just an emotion of sorrow, but a profound change of heart, a decision to turn away from the path of disobedience, back to the ways laid down by God. For the Bible, the stimulus to repentance is the love of God, which stirs in the sinner the feelings that lead to the action of decision. (See also **penance**; **sackcloth**.)

Requiem

A special Mass in the Roman Catholic Church, offered for the dead. Although in the first instance a liturgical form for use by worshippers in the normal course of church life, it has been developed into a particular musical form, such as the Requiems by Mozart and Benjamin Britten. (See also **Mass**.)

restore

A notion which runs through the writings of the Old and New Testaments: the desire to see God bring back both the lost glory of Israel and the lost innocence of mankind. The longing to see God, through Christ, bringing back the whole of creation to its initial state lies behind the future hope implicit in the Gospel. (See also **Israel**.)

resurrection

The rising again after death of all humanity. The doctrine of resurrection came late to Israel, not developing until the period of the Exile. No theology of individual survival is clearly set out in the Old Testament, and even as late as the time of Christ, there was heated debate between pressure groups within Judaism as to the whole issue of life after death. The Sadducees refuted the notion, while the Pharisees advocated it. The New Testament, in the light of the Church's experience of Easter and her faith in the risen Christ, writes the doctrine of resurrection into the very heart of its beliefs, with the key ingredient being a deep conviction about the bodily resurrection of Jesus. Resurrection is there stated as miracle – not as some kind of natural process that comes from the inherent immortality of the soul, but as a new possibility brought into being by Christ's resurrection, and made available as his gift to humanity. There is a clear assumption that this resurrection will be a resurrection of the body, not some abstract spiritualized essence, but recognizably the individual who dies, raised with a new spiritual body. The whole theology and hope of resurrection in the New Testament hinges on the miracle of Easter morning. As St Paul argues: 'if Christ be not raised, then your faith is in vain'. (See also **Resurrection of Jesus**; **soul**.)

Resurrection of Jesus

The fundamental conviction of the early Church, that Jesus of Nazareth was raised to life on the third day after his crucifixion by the power of God as a demonstration of the success of his mission to save the world. Apart from this belief, there was no purpose or reason for the Church, and it was the experience of the risen Jesus which transformed his disciples into the courageous witnesses who became the Church. The Gospels record the discovery of an empty tomb, and some of them speak of encounters with a risen Jesus experienced by the disciples, with clear indications that this was not a ghostly apparition, but a resurrected saviour. The significance of the event is much discussed in the New Testament, for it is seen as proof positive of the unique status of Jesus as the Messiah, and the foundation of the hope of eternal life for the believer. (See also **Ascension**; **resurrection**.)

revelation

An act of making known; the fundamental assumption of the Old and New Testaments, that we only know of God what he chooses to tell us or show us through prophets, writers, and in creation. This is in contrast with the view that man can by searching find out all he wants to know about God. Revelation happens in a variety of ways and situations such as dreams, heavenly envoys (angels), religious encounters between God and particular individuals (such as Moses at the burning bush), and the order and consistency of the natural world. He reveals himself, too, in the teaching of the Law, in the rebuke of inspired prophets, and in the story of his people Israel and their journey. For the New Testament, Christ himself is seen as the supreme and complete revelation of God. (See also **Bible**; **Revelation, Book of**; **vision**.)

Revelation, Book of

A book of the Bible within the tradition of apocalyptic literature, written to a specific situation of pressure and persecution with a view to inspiring hope, assurance, and courage. It is not, as some would have it, a timetable describing with calculating accuracy the future of the world. Using striking symbols, many of which would be understood completely by the contemporary churches to whom the book is addressed, the writer describes a catalogue of visions pointing to the end of time, and the ultimate victory of the faithful Christians and the glorious triumph of Christ. (See also **apocalypse**; **Four Horsemen of the Apocalypse**; **revelation**.)

revival

The reawakening of spiritual enthusiasm which has lain dormant within a community or nation. There have been a whole series of religious revivals throughout the history of the Church when, often inspired by the powerful preaching of individuals, a great reawakening of latent spirituality occurs, and many who have had little interest in the life and worship of the Church are fired by a new spiritual energy and commitment. (See also **charismatic movement**; **evangelical**; **preaching**.)

righteous

In human terms, an individual's personal integrity, uprightness, and moral correctness before law and society; in a theological sense, the standing of an individual in the eyes of God. For the Bible, the conviction is that no one measures up to the expectations of a holy God, and cannot thus be 'put right' (made righteous) with God without divine help. For the Jews, this was made possible through the rigours of the sacrificial system. For the New Testament writers, it was made possible through the work of Jesus. (See also **sacrifice**.)

Roman Catholicism

The doctrine, worship, and life of the Roman Catholic Church. A direct line of succession is claimed from the earliest Christian communities, centring on the city of Rome, where St Peter (claimed as the first bishop of Rome) was martyred. The Church was the only effective agency of civilization in Europe, and after the 11th-century schism with the Byzantine or Eastern Church, it was the dominant force in the Western world, the Holy Roman Empire. The Protestant Reformation of the 16th-century inspired revival, and the need to restate doctrine in an unambiguous form and to purge the church and clergy of abuses and corruption was recognized. The most dramatic reforms were enacted by the two Vatican Councils of the 19th and 20th centuries.

Doctrine is declared by the Pope, or by a General Council with the approval of the Pope, and is summarized in the Nicene Creed. Scripture is authoritative, and interpreted by the *magisterium* or teaching office of the Church. The tradition of the Church is also accepted as authoritative, special importance being attributed to the early church fathers and to the medieval scholastics, notably St Thomas Aquinas. Principal doctrines are similar to those of mainstream Protestant and Orthodox Churches – God as Trinity, creation, redemption, the person and work of Jesus Christ and the place of the Holy Spirit – the chief doctrinal differences being the role of the Church in salvation, and its sacramental theology. Ancient traditional practices such as the veneration of the Virgin Mary and the Saints, or the Stations of the Cross, are still regarded as valuable aids to devotion. (See also **Christianity**; **Pope**; **Thomism**; **Vatican Councils**.)

Rosary

A sequence of prayers recited using a string of beads, or a knotted cord, each bead or knot representing one prayer in the series. In Christianity the Rosary is the Rosary of the Blessed Virgin Mary – a series of prayers, using beads, which includes one Our Father, ten Hail Mary's, and one Glory Be To The Father. Each series is called a *decade*, which is recited fifteen times in the full form, or five times in the shorter version, each decade being a meditation upon some aspect of the life of Christ or the Virgin Mary herself. This popular method of structured and directed prayer dates from the 13th century. (See also **prayer**.)

Rosicrucianism

An esoteric religious order, derived from the thought of Christian Rosenkreutz (born c.1378); also called the *Order of the Rosy Cross*. The movement emerged following the anonymous publication of two pamphlets in Germany in 1614/15, which gave an account of Rosenkreutz and his discoveries of occult and alchemical secrets found on his travels to the East. The pamphlets encouraged men of learning to join and share in these secrets. Though intended to be satirical, the pamphlets were taken seriously, and led to the development of a variety of occult organizations. (See also **occultism**.)

S

Sabbath

The special day of rest for Jews, designated particularly for the worship of God. Falling on the seventh day of the week, the Sabbath requires the cessation from all work, for it is understood in the Old Testament to be an echo of the seventh day of creation, when God 'rested' from his creative endeavours. Recognizing the Sabbath restrictions became a distinctive feature of Judaism. 'Sabbath observance' remains an important idea in the collective community spirit of certain regions of the British Isles, the Sabbath principle being applied strictly to Sunday and to 'Lord's Day' observance. The shift from the seventh to the first day of the week as the special day of worship became a distinguishing feature of the life of the Christian Church, setting it quite definitely in contrast to the practices of Judaism. (See also **worship**.)

sabbatical year

The idea presented in the Old Testament that the land, no less than the people who farm it, needs a rest – in this case in every seventh year. The land is to be left fallow, to provide for its continued good health and for the ongoing benefit of the natural order. Along with this 'green' idealism went the commitment in the seventh year to free all Hebrew slaves, unless they chose to remain on a permanent basis with their master. Furthermore, debts between Israelites were to be cancelled and suspended in the sabbatical cycle of years. It is not clear from the Old Testament account that these radical and humane ideals were widely adhered to in practice. The notion survives (again, often in theory rather than practice) in the conception of a period of research leave granted to a university teacher at regular intervals.

sack cloth

A rough cloth made from goat's hair, often worn as a sign of sorrow or regret in Old Testament times. A working person's cloth, it represented simplicity and poverty. With religious symbolism it was worn during mourning or at a time of repentance for sin, as a way of humbling oneself before God. (See also **repentance**.)

Sacrament

A ritual observance in Christian worship in which a visible, external act signifies an internal spiritual grace. While Orthodox and Roman Catholic Churches enjoy seven such sacred rites – baptism, confirmation, the Eucharist (Communion), penance (reconciliation), anointing the sick (extreme unction), ordination, and marriage – Protestant Churches generally recognize only baptism and Communion as sacraments. Participation in the Sacraments is a response of obedience to the command of Christ, and they are presented to the believer as a special means of grace which can deepen faith. (See also **anointing the sick**; **baptism**; **Confirmation**; **Eucharist**; **Orders, Holy**; **penance**.)

sacrifice

An offering to a god, from earliest times widely practised in many different religions. In the pagan cultures that surrounded the people of Israel, sacrifices were performed to appease the anger of a wrathful god. By contrast, the Israelites saw them as a way of telling the people something about themselves and about God himself. Certain sacrifices were connected with harvest time, and the recognition of God as the true author of the harvest. The giving up of the first fruits of the harvest illustrated God's ultimate claim upon all things. Sacrifices were also used to denote the seriousness of an agreement: if it was sealed with blood, the commitment was special. However, it is as a way of dealing with sin, and of God's reaction to sin, that the Jewish sacrificial system comes into its own. In his love, God allows another to stand in place of the sinner; the sacrifice dies the death which, because of the seriousness of sin, the sinner should die. For Christians, within this framework, Christ is understood to be the perfect sacrifice, offered once for everyone, and for all time. (See also **altar**; **atonement**; **blood**; **burnt-offering**; **expiate**; **propitiation**; **redemption**.)

Sadducees

A priestly group within Judaism, taking their name from the Old Testament high priest of David's reign, Zadok. They were a theologically conservative group of intellectuals, who, at the time of Christ, had significant influence within the national life of Israel, largely because of their willingness to cooperate with the occupying forces of the Roman Empire. They saw themselves as in opposition to the Pharisees, in particular over the issue of resurrection, which they took to be a new philosophy absent from mainstream Judaism. The Sadducees felt the same threat from Jesus as the Pharisees, and the alliance between the two parties worked to bring about the Crucifixion. Like much of Jewish culture, the Sadducees and their theology did not survive the fall of Jerusalem in AD 70. (See also **Judaism**; **Pharisees**.)

saint

Originally, a way of speaking of any holy person or heavenly messenger. The New Testament applied the word to any member of the Christian Church, and ordinary Christians are clearly so designated in the Epistles of Paul. Later, the title came to be reserved for people who were especially devout, heroic, or successful within the life and mission of the Church. It became accepted practice to turn to particular saints as a means of help and intercession. The practice was unacceptable to the 16th-century reformers, but persisted in the Orthodox and Roman Catholic Churches, where there are now many definite and rigorous criteria by which eligibility for sainthood (*canonization*) is judged. (See also **canonization**.)

salvation

Deliverance from the power and effects of sin. Throughout the Bible, God is the initiator of the action that saves – whether it be a crisis for the nation, community, or individual. In New Testament theology, the spiritual health of mankind is in a state of crisis because of sin. In response to this plight, God's initiative brings Jesus Christ to rescue humanity in the costly experience of incarnation, death, and resurrection. As a result of his action, the dreaded experience of death is transformed into the gateway to eternal life, and the judgement and condemnation of a holy God has been absorbed and satisfied by Jesus Christ. The status of mankind is now that of having been 'saved'. (See also **atonement**; **elect, the**; **judgement**; **predestination**; **Saviour**; **universalism**; **works**.)

Salvation Army

An organization founded in London in 1865 by William Booth (1829–1912), to offer a Christian response of practical concern for the needy and poor of the city. It is a non-sectarian Christian movement, with a strong evangelical flavour, and organized along a pseudo-military structure, with a distinctive uniform and a series of ranks of seniority. The Salvation Army is found in over 80 countries and retains a place of special regard in the minds of ordinary people for its band music and for its magazine *War Cry*, traditionally sold in the busy pubs of large cities by members of the Army who, as they sell, collect money for the support of their charity work. (See also **evangelical**.)

sanctify

To set apart for a sacred purpose. The desire to make things holy lies behind the notion of sanctification. The sacrifices brought to the Temple had to be made holy, set apart for God, dedicated to his use and purposes. The aim of the Christian is to be made holy, to find such a degree of commitment to God that all other distractions will hold no appeal. A life of purity and love for God will be the visible expression of that degree of devotion. (See also **holy**.)

sanctuary

(1) A place of shelter where the innocent, or even the guilty, can go and be guaranteed safety and protection, even from the forces of law; more broadly, a place where rest, recuperation, and shelter from the elements is offered in the name of God – where hospitality and true charity are given without question to the needy individual.

(2) A special place designated and reserved for the worship of God or (in pagan religions) gods. The places where the God of Israel was worshipped took a variety of forms. The tent called the Tabernacle which went with the Israelites during their nomadic period was their special focal point of worship. It was later replaced by the Temple of Solomon. The idea of a sanctuary as a designated place remains today; the main area in a church is known as the sanctuary – a place where sacred things are done, seen, and heard, and where the sensibilities of the religious can find security and peace of expression. (See also **Tabernacle**; **worship**.)

Sanhedrin

The main decision-making and policy-making council of the Jews in Biblical times. It emerged as the strong priestly element in political and religious life during the time of Greek occupation in the 3rd and 2nd centuries BC. The high priest played a major role in its deliberations, and the major influence within it was the Sadducee party. The great council of the Sanhedrin held ultimate authority within Judaism on all religious matters relating to Jewish law, and this gave them enormous power. While the power to pass the death sentence was, by the time of Christ, reserved for the Roman authorities, the Sanhedrin did have powers of arrest and trial as seen in Gospel narrative. The role of the Sanhedrin ceased with the fall of Jerusalem and the destruction of Jewish life in AD 70. (See also **Judaism**.)

Satan

A Hebrew word for the adversary of God, also known as the *Devil*. A crystallized view of a personalized devil figure came late to Jewish thought, perhaps through Persian influence, or even simply through the harsh experience of their history. Since it could hardly be God who is the author of evil, there must – the argument runs – be another force or personality, ultimately under the power of God, yet apparently free to the point of tempting individuals, and bringing chaos to individual lives. The consensus of Biblical views of Satan is to see him as the main enemy of human aspirations, though his power is always acknowledged to be partial. (See also **angel**; **demon**; **Satanism**; **serpent**.)

Satanism

The worship of Satan or of demons, often involving the deliberate perversion of familiar Christian ritual, and the practice of witchcraft and occultism. The appeal to dark spiritual forces burgeoned in the 19th century and there is evidence of a significant revival of interest in Satanism in the present day. Its appeal lies in its overturning and attacking the taboos implicit in normal Christian practice. (See also **Satan**.)

Saviour

A title applied to Jesus, widely used today within the Christian Church to indicate the purpose of his coming into the world.

The idea that God saves his people is a significant one, though the specific title of 'saviour' does not appear much in the New Testament. This surprising restraint may be to do with the many so-called 'saviours' who emerged from time to time in the ancient world with their bogus claims to put the world to rights. The New Testament writers, while acknowledging the purpose of Jesus coming to earth to be that of procuring salvation for all, would not have wanted Christ to be confused with such individuals, and perhaps for that reason made little use of the term. (See also **salvation**.)

scapegoat

One of two goats which, on the Day of Atonement, had symbolically placed upon them the sins of the people of Israel. The scapegoat was then, according to Leviticus 16, sent out into the wilderness, to carry the sins of the people into a kind of symbolic oblivion and forgottenness. The second goat was sacrificed. The origins of this vivid portrayal of the loosing of the excess baggage of past guilts and the whole year's regrets and failures, lie in obscurity, but the symbolism remains effective. The term is still in use in the sense of someone who has to carry the condemnation that would normally fall on the guilty. (See also **atonement**.)

scarlet

A colour used in the decorated curtains and wall hangings in the Holy Tabernacle of Israel's worship, and specifically too in the vestments worn by the priest. On one level, like purple, scarlet was an indication of wealth and status. It also became associated with the symbolism of sin and cleansing. The Bible affirms that 'though your sins be as scarlet, they shall be as white as snow', contrasting the vivid dark stain of the scarlet dye, indelible and undeniable, with the dazzling whiteness of purity.

Scientology

A cult, developed in the 1950s by science-fiction writer Ron Hubbard (1911–86), which he declared would free the minds of its followers to understand the great truths of existence, and give them a sense of control over their own lives. Although Jesus is invoked as one of history's great teachers, Scientology, while calling itself a 'church', owes no allegiance to mainstream Christian belief. Its methods, and its message of self-discovery and pseudo-scientific jargon have raised deep controversy. Its financial management, and its disturbing power over its followers, have led to a series of law-suits and exposures in the media.

scribes

A class of men who emerged in the period following the exile in Babylon, whose task was to interpret and preserve the law of God, maintaining the great traditions of Judaism. Their explanations, in turn, became a feature of Jewish thought and opinion, and often developed a significance almost equal to the law itself. While many of these men were genuine seekers after the will of God, by the time of Jesus some seemed to have become ensnared by their own narrow tradition, and thus found themselves in conflict with his dynamic, liberated message. Christ's charge of hypocrisy levelled against them meant that their opposition to his ministry was inevitable. (See also **Judaism**.)

Scriptures

A term applied specifically to the writings of the Old Testament, in the first instance, and later to the Bible as a whole. These writings were considered to express the word of God to his people in special revelation – and thus provided the inspiration for the committed follower. Within the religious life of both Judaism and Christianity, the Scriptures have a clear authority for the formation of theology, the development of doctrine, and the defining of religious practice. Many religions, also, have a body of sacred writing which believers revere as scriptural. (See also **Bible**; **inspiration**.)

Scrolls, Dead Sea

See **Dead Sea Scrolls**

sect

A religious body which has broken away from a main body of believers and is often regarded as extreme or heretical by them. Sects have the distinguishing characteristic of accepting enough of the main corpus of belief to be recognizable as a spin-off from the established body, but having sufficient differences not to be wholly identified with it. They are convinced of the correctness of their own point of view, and maintain that they (and not the established body) are the ones who have kept true to the authentic beliefs of the parent religion. There is, accordingly, always some key element of belief which needs to be affirmed before an individual may join the group. In the New Testament the main sects were the Pharisees and the Sadducees. Christianity was initially thought to be a sect of Judaism until its radical identity became clear and it stood quite apart. However, very soon – as seems to happen with all religions – differences of opinion, priority, and direction began to appear within Christianity, and sects developed within it no less than in other religions. (See also **cult**; **Pharisees**; **religion**; **Sadducees**.)

selah /'si:lə/
A musical term frequently used in the Book of Psalms, whose meaning is not entirely clear. It is thought to be a signal to the Temple singers to sing a chorus or doxology; or perhaps to the Temple musicians to play in a particular way during a pause from the singing.

Septuagint
A pre-Christian Greek version of the Jewish Scriptures, edited by Jewish scholars and later adopted by Greek-speaking Christians. The name derives from the Latin for 'seventy', referring to the 72 Jewish academics who did the work of translation, traditionally thought to be in the 3rd century BC. The Septuagint served as the key text for the early Church, which explains why quotations in the New Testament of Old Testament texts are found in the Septuagint translation. (See also **Bible**.)

seraphim
Celestial creatures, with six wings but an appearance of humanness, who serve in the courts of heaven and announce the glory and holiness of God. Since they appear only in the dramatic vision of Isaiah, it is unclear whether they are features of the hierarchy of angels in a more developed angelology, or simply

products of a particular writer's particular experience, attempting to convey the sense of fire and lightning which emanates from the holiness of God. (See also **angel**; **cherub**.)

serpent

A snake-like creature which features frequently in the symbolism and myths of religion. In the Bible, the serpent appears as a symbol of healing (eg Numbers 21) and of wisdom (eg Matthew 10), but predominantly as a symbol of evil (Genesis) with its power to entice people away from loyalty to God. The serpent tricks Eve into a betrayal of God's will, and ensuing emnity develops between humanity and snake. The serpent is seen to represent the attractiveness of sin, and is responsible for wrecking humanity's innocence. It can thus be seen how the identification of the serpent with Satan occurred – Satan using the guise of the serpent to perform his evil work. The Book of Revelation reinforces this identification, specifically describing Satan as the 'ancient serpent'. The theological idea of Christ, the second Adam, achieving a triumph over Satan, echoes the Garden of Eden and the abject failure of the first Adam to deal with the serpent's wiles. (See also **Satan**.)

Shakers

An American sect, founded in England in the 18th century by psychic visionary Ann Lee (1736–84); more correctly known as the United Society for Believers in Christ's Second Appearing. They take their name from the ecstatic dancing which forms part of their worship. The Shakers believe that Christ himself has appeared with Ann Lee, giving her message a particular authority. In philosophy they are pacifist, and choose to live in a community together. The practice of strict celibacy, which is a fundamental ingredient of their belief and practice, has caused their numbers to fall to such a degree they have all but ceased to exist.

Shekinah or Shechinah /ʃɛˈkaɪnə/

An important idea in Hebrew thought, referring to the presence of God in a special involvement with his people, Israel. Particular places were associated with this special presence, such as Moses's burning bush on Mount Sinai, or the Holy of Holies in the Tabernacle in the wilderness. The symbolism of light and glory is used to express this idea of the nearness of God, and the reality that he accompanies his people on their journey.

Shema /ʃəˈmɑː/

A popular ancient prayer of the Jews, dating at least from the 2nd century AD, and using words from the Old Testament (Deuteronomy 6. 4–9, 11. 13–21, and Numbers 15. 37–41). The name derives from the Hebrew verb 'hear' with which the prayer opens: 'Hear, O Israel, the Lord our God is one'. Jewish morning and evening prayers are begun with the Shema, coming before the Amidah. It can be recited in any language, and with its emphasis on the oneness of God, and because of its universal use by Jewish worshippers, it has a unifying effect within the community of Judaism.

shepherd

A classic Biblical metaphor which explains the character of God and the nature of his caring relationship with his people. A crucial factor in the survival of a nomadic people, sheep – used for clothing, food, and milk – were a precious commodity, and because of their value to the Israelites, their use in sacrifice gave the act seriousness and meaning. The shepherd played a vital role in the care of the sheep, leading them to new pasture land and providing refreshment and protection, and the theology emerges naturally of God's care and provision being of a similar kind. While God, and later Jesus, has the title of shepherd attributed to him, people are seen by the poets and prophets of Israel to be as scatter-brained and prone to wandering off as are sheep. Add to the imagery the notion of Jesus as a sacrificial lamb, spoken of as 'the lamb of God who takes away the sin of the world', and we have the whole richness of an imagery that would, to nomadic people, be clear, vivid, and significant. (See also **lamb**.)

Sheol /ˈʃiːoʊl/

The place of the dead in early Hebrew thought. It was conceived of as a neutral location, without the overtones of punishment we now associate with ideas of 'hell-fire and damnation', and is perhaps more accurately thought of as a kind of 'waiting-room in eternity', where the spirits of the departed go to be sorted out. The idea was not carried over into New Testament thinking. (See also **hell**.)

shibboleth

A word used to identify Gileadites from Ephraimites, during a war in the early days of the settlement in Canaan (Judges 12. 1–6), The inability of the Ephraimites to pronounce correctly the word *shibboleth* was used as a means of identification of members of that particular group. The idea has carried over into modern idiom to mean the slogans or catch-phrases which specifically identify the members of a particular group.

Shinto

The religion native to Japan, whose roots lie in the ancient folk religions and nature worship of the earliest days of Japanese culture. In the 8th century, it was necessary to distinguish between Buddhism and this indigenous religion, which led to the adoption of the name Shinto, meaning 'the way of *Kami*, or sacred power'. Though it borrowed many elements from Buddhism, its appeal to the mysterious powers of nature, and its desire for the benevolence and protection of those powers, made it distinct. The Imperial family was designated to have divine powers, and state Shinto developed, with reverence, loyalty, and obedience to the divine Emperor. By the 19th century, it was necessary to separate Shrine Shinto from Sectarian Shinto, with the former being regarded as a state cult, and the latter seen as a religion, though not eligible for state support. The defeat of Japan in World War 2 brought an end to the official status of State Shinto. (See also **Mikado**.)

Shiva

One of the three principal Gods of Hinduism. He is a God of contrasting characteristics – creation and destruction, good and evil, fertility and asceticism. He is also considered to be the original Lord of Dance, and in Hindu symbolism is represented most usually as a phallic emblem, indicating the power of procreation. (See also **Kali**.)

shofar /ˈʃoʊfə/

The Hebrew word for a special ram's horn, blown as a musical instrument on high days and holy days. It is used to summon in the Jewish New Year, and to mark the end of the Day of

Atonement. In wartime, in Biblical days, it was used to announce important news.

shrine

A special focal point of worship in a particular locality. In the Bible, the word refers particularly to the inner sanctuary of the Temple at Jerusalem. It also has overtones of pagan practices, where household gods might be located in a niche in a home, or out in the countryside, drawing worshippers to sacred places within the cult of a specific god or goddess. In modern usage, the term is usually applied to a holy place, especially one connected with pilgrimages (such as at Lourdes or Fatima), or to a sacred image or relic kept within a church or other religious building. (See also **worship**.)

Sikhism

A religion founded by the Guru Nanak in the Punjab area of North India in the 16th century. It is a religion of the Gurus, and its continuance is due to the successful influence of a series of nine Gurus who succeeded Nanak and kept Sikhism alive. God is considered the true Guru, who brings his word to mankind through the ten historical Gurus. This line ended in 1708, since which time the Sikh community is called 'Guru'. Their sacred scripture, the Adi Granth, also has the authority of a Guru. (See also **Guru**.)

simony

The practice of trading religious objects or benefits for money; in particular, in the medieval Church, the business of selling indulgences, or guarantees of divine forgiveness. The name derives from the Samaritan sorcerer Simon Magus, referred to in Acts of the Apostles 8. 9–24 as one who tried to buy spiritual powers. This corruption of religious ideals made the Roman Catholic Church acutely susceptible to criticism, and was a major causative factor of the 16th-century Reformation. (See also **indulgences**; **Reformation**.)

sin

A turning away from God. According to the Bible, sin is mankind's biggest problem, the whole drama of salvation occurring as a response to that problem. Because sin is an attitude of people, the result of their free choice, sinners find their whole existence threatened by the consequences of punishment and separation which follow from it. The sacrificial system was instituted as a way of dealing with the seriousness of sin, and in the New Testament this is taken a step further: the purpose of Jesus is to fulfil and supersede the old sacrificial system, removing the threat of sin. (See also **Fall, the; grace; justification; original sin; sacrifice; sin-offering; temptation**.)

sin-offering

A sacrifice designated to cover those sins of which a worshipper was genuinely unaware, but which were none the less real, requiring attention. Old Testament Law recognized the need to provide a means of making sure that even sins done in forgetfulness or ignorance might be removed from the list of accusations against the sinner. A sin-offering was a ritualistic safety-net, which ensured that nothing was left unforgiven. (See also **sin**.)

Social Gospel

A movement which aimed to translate the meaning of the Christian Gospel into action and philosophy that could relate to the social and political issues of modern life. It began in America in c.1870, its main proponents being Washington Gladdon (1836–1918), Walter Rauschenbusch (1861–1918), and Shailer Matthews (1863–1941). It represented an attempt to 'earth' the Gospel in the real issues of the world, and was seen to be a challenge both to the abstract concerns of academic theology and to the evangelical obsession with narrow notions of personal salvation. (See also **Gospel**.)

Son of God

In the Old Testament any individual who is noted for enjoying a specially intimate connection with God. The nation of Israel was itself called by God 'my Son' (Hosea 11.1) The idea was applied in the New Testament to Jesus – not so much because he used it of himself, but as a clear implication of the special relationship he claimed between himself and God the Father. Jesus himself preferred the enigmatic title 'Son of Man'. Paul however, following his enlightening experience of the risen Jesus, had no hesitation in giving him the title 'Son of God', and the frequent references in the Gospels to Jesus being addressed by God as 'beloved son' suggests that it is appropriate. Additional justification is given to the idea by the parables of Jesus, notably the Parable of the Vineyard, where a clear, qualitative distinction is drawn between the prophets, servants, and spokesmen of God, and the son who comes in his Father's name. It was this distinction, so specifically made, which enraged Jesus' critics, and brought the charge of blasphemy down upon him. (See also **God**; **Trinity**.)

Son of Man

A title Jesus prefers to use for himself. The notion can be traced back to the Old Testament where, in the later books, the 'Son of Man' is spoken of as one in whom the New Age of God's Kingdom will reside (see especially Daniel 7. 13). It is part of Jesus's strategy to hold back from a direct claim to be the Messiah, but to convey the enigma of his true identity and purpose in a way which would identify himself in the Jewish mind with the coming glory and at the same time with the whole of humanity.

soteriology

The academic discipline in theology which examines the nature of the work of Jesus Christ in saving the world – the role of Jesus as Saviour. It has been a major preoccupation of theologians since the earliest beginnings of the Church.

soul

The notion of a personal self, recognized as in some way able to have a life apart from its purely physical manifestation. The Bible is unwilling to drive a wedge between body and soul, designating one bad and the other good, as some religions do. The integrity of the personality is seen to involve all aspects of humanity – physical, mental, and spiritual. The commitment of the New Testament to this view is expressed in the doctrine of the resurrection of the body. (See also **resurrection**.)

spirit

The non-material reality of the personality. It is not simply the mechanics of thinking and acting, but the choosing, responsible, growing or diminishing self which relates and loves. The metaphors of breath and wind lie behind the Biblical idea of spirit. The breath which indicates the presence of life is thought to be an echo of God's breathing of life into humanity at creation; while the mysterious power of the wind is used as an image of the principle of life that lies in each person, the absence of which means death. (See also **Holy Spirit**.)

Stations of the Cross

A series of fourteen pictures or wooden carvings depicting the events and incidents of the Passion of Christ, showing the story from the time of his being condemned through to his death and burial. They are a familiar sight in Roman Catholic and some Anglican churches. Some of the events illustrated are not found in Scripture, but the Stations of the Cross serve as an aid to prayer and are a popular form of pious devotion.

stigmata

Marks or wounds which appear on a person's body, replicating the wounds of Christ at his crucifixion. Throughout the story of the Church, there have been individuals who manifest these features. The stigmata may occur only on occasion, at times of great spiritual intensity, or may be a permanent feature. They are considered to be an indication of a form of miraculous identification with, and sharing in, the sufferings of Christ. (See also **miracle**.)

stoning

The accepted form of capital punishment in Israel in Biblical times. It was recommended for a whole range of offences, 17 in all, covering a wide spectrum from murder to the breaking of the Sabbath.

stupa /ˈstuːpə/

A mound built to mark the site containing the ashes of some great individual – a leader or spiritual guide, such as the Buddha himself. Stupas later came to house the remains of Buddhist monks and other items of religious significance. Originally from India, they were the precursors of the pagoda. (See also **pagoda**.)

suffering

One of the great mysteries which religion attempts to address – in particular, the issue of 'innocent' suffering. The Old Testament considers that suffering is in some way tied up with human sin – that there is a causal connection between human disobedience to the will of God, and the consequent suffering encountered in human experience. However, the suffering of the innocent is not fully explained by the Old Testament, which concludes that faith is the only response to what is essentially a mystery. The New Testament reveals a Jesus who in the name of God directs his power and love against suffering. A particularly Roman Catholic response is to see it as an opportunity to receive and experience a special portion of God's grace – thus turning a negative into a creative positive. In this view, suffering bravely borne, or willingly entered in upon, brings glory in witness and a deepened experience of God. The Biblical vision of a future devoid of suffering is a clear indication that suffering represents a denial of God's will, and that one of the goals of the salvation he achieves in Christ is to obliterate suffering from the experience of his people.

Sun Dance

In the traditional religion of American Indians, a ceremony or festival lasting from two to five days, at which the dancers produced in themselves a trance-like state by gazing at the Sun. Several rituals involved self-inflicted pain, such as piercing the chest with skewers attached to a sacred pole; this, they believed, endued them with great spiritual power.

Sunday

In Christian tradition the first day of the week, seen as a day of rest and religious observance; the name was borrowed from pagan Sun worship. A key feature which identified the early Church as something more than simply a new sect within Judaism was the radical step of shifting the day of worship away from the Jewish Sabbath to the first day of the week, in recollection of the day of Christ's Resurrection. In keeping Sunday as the first day, the Church now finds itself out of tune with contemporary social practice, as the International Standards Organization's recommendation is for Monday to be the first day – agreed by Britain in 1971. (See also **Sabbath**; **worship**.)

Sunday School

Separate Christian instruction on a Sunday for children within the life of the Church. Sunday Schools are a relatively recent development, the first charity school being set up in 1780 to provide a basic education for poor children.

sweat lodge

The ritual in which North American Indians achieve a purification of body and spirit. The spiritual leader takes those involved into a specially constructed building where they sit around a mound of very hot stones. Prayers and sacred songs are recited as water is poured over the stones.

synagogue

The house of worship and communal centre of a Jewish congregation. When the great Temple at Jerusalem was destroyed in 587 BC and the people were dispersed, the need arose for a focal point of worship and teaching for devout Jews. By the time of Christ, most major cities in the Roman Empire would feature a synagogue. Although the Law of Moses laid down no clear guidelines as to what should happen in synagogue worship, a pattern emerged and became normal practice. The main emphasis lay in reading the ancient scriptures, with the key ideas being expounded, while worship took the form of reciting the Law and the chief liturgical items of Jewish devotion – the Shema, blessings, and prayers. To a widely-scattered and culturally isolated race, the development of the synagogue was a major ingredient in shaping identity, and preserving a sense of their uniqueness as God's chosen people. (See also **Judaism**; **worship**.)

T

Tabernacle

(1) In the Old Testament, a tent, constructed according to very specific orders from God, placed in the middle of the community, and containing all the elements required to preserve his essential mystery. At its centre was the holiest place of all, the *Holy of Holies*, the inner sanctuary containing the Ark of the Covenant. All the symbolism of Jewish ritual (offerings, prayers, sacrifices) was carried out in the Tabernacle, which stood as a sign of God's desire to dwell with his chosen people.

(2) In Roman Catholic and Anglo-Catholic churches, a box containing the sacrament, placed on the altar, and a special focus of devotional attention. (See also **Ark of the Covenant; Judaism**.)

taboo

A notion, originating in the Tonga Islands, which expresses the idea of something forbidden, separated off, sacred, or prohibited. The concept that places and things have to be treated with special respect and care is a common theme in religions all over the world. If the taboo is breached, there is defilement or threat of punishment.

Taizé /ˈteɪzeɪ/

A community founded in 1940 by members of the Reformed Church in France, based in Lyons. It requires of its members adherence to a rule very similar to that of many monastic orders, though they dress as laymen. The commitment of Taizé is to promote Christian unity by breaking down barriers between Protestants and Catholics. Viewed by an international clientele as a spiritual retreat and focus of mission, by young people in particular, its style of participatory worship, with its strong emphasis on music, has evolved as an attractive expression of Christian faith to a whole new generation. (See also **ecumenism**.)

tantra

A spiritual instruction manual found in Buddhism and Hinduism, used by the devotee under the instruction of a Guru to perform his religious discipline. It contains a wide assortment of aids to devotion such as spells, mantras, meditations, and rituals. (See also **Guru**.)

Taoism

One of the major religions of China, believed to have been founded by Lao Tzu (7th century BC), whose book *Tao Te Ching* is held to be sacred. Taoism has had both popular and philosophical forms. A major preoccupation of the popular form is death, and how to deal with it. Spells and charms are used, along with a wide range of ritualistic practices, from spiritualism to priestly activity. Philosophical Taoism, by contrast, uses a mystical approach which attempts to harmonize soul and mind in quietness with the ultimate reality, which is Tao. This requires an emptying of the self from all self-awareness and self-tainted desires, and finding a state of effortless availability

Targum

An Aramaic translation of the Hebrew Scriptures, produced in the 1st century BC. Originally an oral translation of the texts read out in synagogues, it was given a written form during the Rabbinic period. (See also **Old Testament**.)

tefillin /tɛfɪˈliːn/

Two leather cube-shaped containers for key Old Testament texts which are worn, bound over the head and arms, by devout Jews. The practice is in obedience to the Mosaic prescription that the Word of the Law was to be 'a sign upon your head or frontlets before your eyes'. They are worn by Orthodox Jews during morning prayers, except on the Sabbath and at Festivals. (See also **phylacteries**.)

teleological argument

One of the traditional arguments which attempt to prove the existence of God; from Greek *telos*, 'end' or 'purpose'. Its basic thrust is that, since the world in all its structure demonstrates order and purpose, there must be an intelligent, creative force responsible for it. (See also **God**.)

Temple, Jerusalem

The central place of Jewish worship in Old Testament times. Although the Tabernacle had served the people adequately during their nomadic phase, something more substantial was required once they had settled. Jerusalem was chosen as the site of the Temple by King Solomon, having served as capital city during David's time, and standing as it did in a position effectively neutral and so acceptable to both northern and southern kingdoms. The design of the Temple illustrates many features of Israel's culture and theology, such as the exclusive areas for ceremonial washings, inner areas for worship, and the Holy of Holies containing the sacred Ark of the Covenant. After standing for almost 400 years, the Temple was destroyed in the fall of Jerusalem in 587 BC. A second Temple was built on the ancient site following the return of the exiles from Babylon (after 520 BC). There was no possibility of recreating either the former glory or the traditional importance of the original; poverty restricted the grandeur of the structure and the Ark of Covenant had disappeared. This Temple was desecrated by Antiochus Epiphanes in 168 BC, and all that was in it had to be reconsecrated and renewed under Judas Maccabeus. A complete programme of rebuilding was carried out by Herod the Great from 19 BC until AD 60, and the grandeur of the original Temple was restored; but it was destroyed again at the fall of Jerusalem in AD 70, and never reconstructed. (See also **Judaism**; **Tabernacle**.)

temptation

The powerful attractiveness of actions or thoughts opposed to God's will, and destructive of moral purity. The appeal to appetites which exist in every person, and which if unrestrained will draw an individual away from loyalty to God, has always been a feature of human experience, according to the Bible. To be tempted is itself an unavoidable reality, but what an individual *does* with the temptation sets the measure of their spiritual strength. Jesus, as part of humanity, is faced with temptation; his response of obedience and faith in God is the example and the inspiration for his followers. An additional sense of the Authorized Version's use of the word is the idea of a test or trial, where the strength of commitment of a believer is revealed by the challenge. This is the sense of the word in the Lord's Prayer, 'Lead us not into temptation', more accurately found in modern translations as 'Do not bring us to the test'. (See also **sin**.)

Ten Commandments

See **Commandments, Ten**

Tertiaries

Men and women who form the Third Order of religious life. They are usually lay people who seek Christian perfection, while living in the world, under the discipline and guidance of one of the religious orders, such as the Franciscans or Dominicans. A 'regular Tertiary' is a member of a community bound by vows. (See also **Orders, Holy**.)

thanksgiving

An appropriate response of gratitude to God and rejoicing for blessings received. Particularly expressed at times of security and bounty, such as deliverance from crisis, or when the harvest has been plentiful, thankfulness is the natural response of individuals who understand their dependence upon the grace and power of God for their survival. In the New Testament this spirit of appreciation is extended to include the praise resulting from an awareness of the salvation achieved by Christ for all the world.

theism

A belief in a single, transcendent and personal divine being, who made the universe and is in some way still involved with it, while not identical with it. Theism is a major ingredient of Judaism, Islam, and Christianity. (See also **atheism**; **deism**; **monotheism**; **pantheism**; **polytheism**.)

theodicy

The defence of God's goodness and omnipotence against arguments based on the existence of evil in the world. Such an apologetic for God's way of organizing his creation has been a preoccupation of philosophers and theologians from the earliest times. (See also **omnipotence**.)

theology

Orderly and disciplined talk about God. There are two main approaches in Christian tradition: *natural theology* studies the way human reason and the evidences of creation can lead to insight and understanding; *revealed theology* studies the way God shows himself to mankind, using Scriptures, miracles, and the incarnation of Jesus. (See also **'Death of God' theology; feminist theology; liberation theology; moral theology; Thomism.**)

theophany

An appearance of God to the people to whom he has chosen to reveal himself. An example is the experience of Moses on Mt Sinai, where he is addressed by God out of the burning bush.

theosophy

Any system of mystical thought, especially one which emphasizes insight obtained from a direct and immediate experience of God. The term has a particular application in its reference to the basic beliefs of the Theosophical Society, founded in New York in 1875 by Madame Blavatsky (1831–91) and Henry Steel Olcott (1832–1907).

Theravada /θɛrəˈveɪdə/

A form of Buddhism which rejects the role of the Bodhisattvas, and is thus distinguished from Mahayana Buddhism. It is found chiefly in South Asia, and dates from the 3rd century BC. (See also **Bodhisattva; Buddhism.**)

Thomism

The philosophical theology which emanates from St Thomas Aquinas, one of the most influential thinkers in the life of the church; also, later schools which developed from his basic thought. Its theological conclusions, emphasizing natural theology as a source of revelation, have remained profoundly influential in Roman Catholic thought, and in 1879 Thomism was declared the official theological stance of Roman Catholicism. As a consequence, there was a reawakening of interest, in the late 19th century, which came to be called *neo-Thomism*. It has remained an influential feature of Roman Catholic and to some degree Anglican theological discourse. (See also **theology**.)

thorn in the flesh

A bodily weakness which afflicted St Paul, and which he prayed
to be rid of, but on discovering that it remained with him,
he sought refuge in the comfort and grace of God, which he
discovered to be 'sufficient for all my need'. The identity of the
weakness is unknown, though speculation includes epilepsy, ma-
laria, cataracts, and stammering. Paul's experience is now used by
other Christians enduring harsh afflictions, who learn the grace
of God's comfort as they continue to live with their disability.

Tirthankara /tɪə'tænkərə/

The 24 heroes of Jainism, who by their teaching and holy lives
taught Jains how to make their way across the stream from the
constraints of physical existence to freedom from the eternal processes of rebirth; the name derives from a Sanskrit word meaning
'ford-maker'. The heroes are also known as the *Jina*, from which
Jains get their name. (See also **Jainism**.)

tithe

The ancient tradition of making an offering to God of one tenth
of one's material wealth. The practice is found very early on
in the Bible, and is seen as a way of acknowledging God's
right over all our possessions, and as a mark of appreciation for
blessings received. It was a normal part of the Jewish experience
of religious life, the money being used to sustain the work of the
priestly order of Levites. The giving of tithes continued into the
Christian era, a tenth part of all the produce of the land being
given to the clergy – a law in England from the early 10th until
the 19th century.

Toc-H

A club offering Christian fellowship to British soldiers serving in
Belgium in 1915. Its unusual name stems from the letters TOC-H
used by army signallers to refer to Talbot House, where the
Christian fellowship was held. The Club is nonsectarian, and has
involved itself in a wide range of social issues.

tonsure

The practice of shaving all or part of the hair, to show that a man
was a monk or cleric. It is still required in some religious orders.

tongues, speaking in

The ecstatic utterance of uncontrolled and seemingly unintelligible sounds; technically called *glossolalia*. The experience of the church at Pentecost in Acts 2 is described as one in which the Apostles are able to address a multilingual crowd in such a way that each person could appreciate what was being said. Other forms of ecstatic utterance are also reported in the New Testament, which recognizes such experiences as gifts of the Holy Spirit – the freedom and joy to express things too deep for words. Speaking in tongues remains a feature of the charismatic wing of the Church, where a major emphasis is placed upon the driving force of the Holy Spirit. (See also **charismatic movement**; **Holy Spirit**.)

total depravity

In Calvinism, the doctrine that the effect of sin on human nature is to bring its corrupting influence into every aspect of being, so that all human powers bear the limitations imposed by sin. Since it is a result of the presence of original sin, a state of total depravity is an unavoidable condition of the human personality. (See also **Calvinism**; **sin**.)

total immersion

A form of baptism in which the candidate is dipped completely in water. It is practised by some branches of the Christian Church (eg Baptists), who argue that sprinkling with water represents a departure from the practice of the early Church. Total immersion signifies the New Testament imagery of a person 'dying' to the old way of life, being 'buried' with Christ, and 'rising' to a new Christian way of life. (See also **baptism**.)

totem

A natural object, or its carved or painted representation, which serves as an emblem of a tribe or family. It has its origins in the religions of the American Indians, where its thrust was the idea of kinship and bonding. A tribe would adopt a particular animal or plant in which its origins were believed to lie, and this then became sacred, giving the tribe a shared identity.

tradition

A pattern of thought or action passed from generation to generation. Any form of religious practice lasting over many centuries
will accrue features and beliefs which are not central to its original
form, but which nonetheless have an accepted importance. For
Judaism these traditions took the form of Rabbinical interpretations of the basic law of God – interpretations which came to
assume a significance virtually equivalent to the importance of
the Law itself. The status of tradition has always been controversial, with some arguing that human traditions which have
grown up around the Law of God can deflect people from
the original truth of that Law. Jesus is one who makes much
of this confusion of tradition and truth. Even by the time of
Paul's letters, traditions had become embedded in the life of the
Christian Church, especially relating to the Eucharist; and as time
passed, authoritative interpretations of doctrines and teachings of
the Church became a dominant feature. It was to the danger of
these traditions superseding the faith in its original simplicity that
the Reformation addressed its concern. (See also **Law, the**.)

Transcendental Meditation

A method of meditation taught by Maharishi Mahesh Yogi, with
its roots in Hinduism. It grew in popularity in Western societies
during the 1960s, when the Yogi taught his technique to the
popular musical group The Beatles. Those who choose to follow
the method are required to meditate for 20 minutes, twice a day,
and it is believed that this will reduce their stress and help them
to find a deep relaxation. (See also **meditation**.)

transfiguration

An event, reported in three of the Gospels, in which Jesus
underwent a brief and dramatic change, revealing his glory,
hitherto concealed, to some of his disciples through a change
in his appearance and with a voice from heaven confirming his
mission. Moses and Elijah also appear in the incident, a symbol
of the Law and the Prophets reaching fulfilment in Jesus. The
bare bones of the account are difficult to understand, and leave
the question unanswered of whether this was an actual event or
a symbolic drama, portraying the sense of discovery of the three
disciples of what was the true nature of Jesus and his mission.
Coming as it does in the context of Jesus's warning about his future

suffering, it may serve as a corrective to the notion of the suffering Messiah, by emphasizing that, even in this suffering, there will be glory and vindication by God.

transubstantiation

A fundamental doctrine of the Roman Catholic Church, which interprets the Eucharist in such a way as to affirm that the elements of bread and wine used in the Sacrament are, by the grace of God, actually converted into the body and blood of Christ; also called the *real presence*. It was a doctrine rejected by the Protestant Reformers, and one which continues to create a deep division within Christianity. (See also **consubstantiation**; **Eucharist**.)

Trappists

An order of Cistercian monks – the Cistercians of the Strict Observance – who refuse meat, fish, and eggs, are devoted to prayer and holiness of life, and take a vow of perpetual silence. Until 1892 the order was based at La Trappe in France, from where the popular name developed. (See also **Cistercians**.)

Tribes of Israel

Twelve tribes who traditionally, are seen to emerge from their roots in the twelve sons of Jacob. Prior to the Settlement in Canaan, the tribes were a loose federation sharing common interests of defence and kinship. Following the conquest of Canaan, each settled on a specific area of the land, with the Levites enjoying a specialist role as the guardians of the priestly responsibility. When the Civil War erupted in 930 BC, ten tribes formed a northern kingdom of Israel, while two adhered to the royalist connection with the House of David, and founded Judah in the south. When the northern kingdom was defeated in 772 BC, the ten tribes were dispersed throughout the Assyrian Empire, and their land was settled by foreigners. To the southern kingdom accordingly, fell the responsibility to preserve the glories and rituals of Judaism. (See also **Israel**; **patriarch**.)

Trimurti /trɪˈmʊəti/

The Hindu triad of Gods, which together demonstrate the cosmic life and function of the supreme being. It consists of Brahma,

Vishnu, and Shiva, with Brahma's role providing a balance between the two principles of preservation and destruction represented by Vishnu and Shiva. (See also **Hinduism**.)

Trinity

In Christian theology, the unity of three persons (Father, Son, and Holy Spirit) in one godhead. A clearly defined doctrine of the Trinity is not found in the New Testament, but emerges in the writings of the early Church. Christians had understood the nature of God as creator and Father, and then encountered Jesus Christ who, as a result of his teaching and resurrection, they needed to describe also as a divine being, the Son of God. They then encountered a third reality, the Holy Spirit, whose power was felt to be the key to the survival of the faith of Christ in the Church wherever it developed. Faced with these realities, the Church sought to draw them together, developing the doctrine of one God working his purposes out in three different expressions of his nature and perfection. (See also **Christianity**; **God**; **Holy Spirit**; **Son of God**.)

truth

To the Hebrew mind, a concept associated with such notions as reliability and unchangeableness in a shifting world, and integrity and faithfulness in individual relationships; to the Greek mind, an underlying reality, as opposed to surface appearances. Both these elements are found in the New Testament. The truth of God is, firstly, the secure faithfulness of his character, the unchanging nature of his Law and his purposes, and a foundation on which to build personal values. Secondly, the truth of Christ is seen to represent the real situation of God's love – an authentic approach to divine reality. In religious thinking, therefore, truth is to do with more than simply factuality; it is a quest for a deeper reality. When Jesus declares 'I am the truth', he invites us to explore his way as an unchanging foundation on whom people can rest the whole of their lives. (See also **Word**.)

Twelve, the

The twelve men summoned by Jesus to be his followers, and to be responsible for proclaiming the Gospel and the Kingdom which he inaugurated; also known as the *Apostles*. Historically, the number is an echo of the twelve tribes of Israel, the original chosen people, in New Testament thought superseded by the new Israel, the Church of Christ. (See also **apostle**; **Tribes of Israel**.)

type

A means of interpreting the Bible, in which certain individuals are thought to evidence a particular likeness to a later individual, or even to an aspect of theology. Adam, for example, might be considered a type of Christ – Adam, the first of the old humanity; Christ, the first of the new humanity. The Passover is a type of the crucifixion. It is unlikely that the writers of the Old Testament ever expected their writings to be used in this way, and while it can be interesting to trace the likenesses in some cases, a simplistic use of typology can be misleading. (See also **Bible**.)

U

unclean meat

A notion which stems from Jewish law that it was forbidden to eat anything with blood in it (because the blood of an animal was believed to contain its life). Anyone who ate such meat was considered to be in a state of impurity in the sight of God. While Jesus made it clear that he was more concerned with matters of inner conscience, the issue of clean and unclean meat remained a live one for Christians, faced with decisions about whether or not to eat meat that had been used in pagan sacrifices. Paul's conviction that this was a peripheral issue is clearly expressed in his letters, and became the prevailing view of the church. (See also **cleanliness**.)

Unification Church

A religious movement founded by the Reverend Sun Myung Moon in Korea in 1954. Its members, commonly known as *Moonies*, base their thinking and beliefs on the teachings of Moon's book *The Divine Principle*, claimed to contain special revelations of truth given to him by God. Unification teaching is that the whole purpose of creation was to establish a perfect family, a dream spoiled by the Fall, and never accomplished until the arrival of the Reverend and Mrs. Moon. An important element in its practice is mass wedding ceremonies of followers, performed by Reverend Moon. Followers of the church are required to dedicate themselves every week. The Church's methods of recruitment, and its extensive business empire, have led to the movement receiving considerable criticism, both from the media, and from the anxious parents of some who have become members.

Unitarians

A religious movement, in many respects similar to mainstream Christianity, but which rejects the doctrine of the Trinity, and does not accept belief in the divinity of Christ. Its members do however share a Christian standpoint and concern on ethical matters. Their roots derive from the Anabaptists at the time of the Reformation. (See also **Anabaptists**.)

universalism

The doctrine that everyone will be saved. It arose from the difficulty which many Christians have with the idea that their loving God could condemn people to Hell for all eternity. It has grown in popularity, especially in modern Protestant theology, because of a desire to show respect for other world faiths which, according to the non-universalist position, are by implication doomed because they have not made a decision to follow Christ. Underlying the belief, too, lies a conviction of the completeness of the salvation won by Christ – a salvation achieved for everyone, not dependent on the understanding or even the acceptance of individuals for its reality. (See also **salvation**.)

Unknown God, The

A hypothetical divinity to whom an altar was dedicated in Athens by the ancient Greeks. St Paul used this dimension of Greek religion to promote the God encountered in Christianity and revealed in Jesus Christ.

Urim and Thummim

The instruments used by the High Priests of Israel to cast lots in order to reach decisions. They are thought to have been two small flat stones, marked with a notation for 'yes' and 'no' or 'good' and 'evil'. These were part of the High Priest's sacred vestments, and were believed to be a useful means of ascertaining God's response to major questions affecting religious or community life. (See also **lots, casting of**.)

Ursulines

A Roman Catholic religious order dedicated to the education of girls. It had its origins in a congregation founded in 1535 by St Angela as 'the company of St Ursula', a legendary 4th-century saint and martyr. (See also **monasticism**.)

usury

The practice of lending money at an exorbitant rate of interest. The issue has often been associated with Jewish culture, and has fostered a caricature of Judaism that has proved damaging to the image of the Jew. The Old Testament expressly forbids the Israelites to make loans to members of their own community, since this created division and possible hardship within a tightly-knit community, but they were permitted to give loans, and charge interest, in dealings with foreigners.

V

Vatican Councils

Two significant Councils of the Roman Catholic Church. The first Vatican Council was called by Pope Pius IX in 1869–70 to attend to crucial matters of doctrine, canon law, church discipline, foreign missions, and the important relations between Church and state. One of its most significant determinations was the formulation of the doctrine of papal infallibility. The Second Vatican Council, called by John XXIII, changed the face of Roman Catholicism in a profound way. The emphasis was upon the renewal of the spiritual life of the Church – reforming liturgical practice, and renewing the structures of the Church for a modern age. Ecumenical in spirit, its influence in forming a new mood for the Roman Catholic Church has been far-reaching and creative. (See also **ecumenism**.)

Veda /ˈveɪdə/

The ancient texts of Hinduism, dating from c. 1500 BC; the name derives from a Sanskrit word meaning 'knowledge'. They comprise four collections called the *Vedas*, the *Brahmanas* appended to them, and the *Aranyakas* and *Upanishads*, which serve as an epilogue or conclusion. In its earliest form the Veda was made up of the Rig-Veda (sacred songs or hymns of praise), the Sama-Veda (special chants and tunes used by priests during sacrifices), and the Yajur-Veda (sacrificial formulae); to these were later added the Athara-Veda (spells, charms, and exorcistic chants). The Aranyakas and Upanishads declare that liberation can be enjoyed without sacrifices, and they introduce the notion of monism – the view that there is a single principle which will unlock the meaning of all things. They were subsequently thought to be the fulfilment of the ideas expressed in the Veda, and came to be called the *Vedanta* ('the end of the Veda'). (See also **Hare Krishna Movement**; **Hinduism**.)

veil

A curtain of embroidered linen in the Holy of Holies which separated the area from the rest of the Tabernacle. A similar curtain was found in the Temple. The New Testament's accounts in Matthew's Gospel affirms that this veil was split in two at the moment of Jesus's death – a sign that Christ, as the true High Priest, had made a way for all mankind into the very presence of God. (See also **Temple, Jerusalem**.)

Vespers

An act of worship found in the Western Church in the late afternoon or evening, consisting of a hymn, psalms, lessons, and various prayers. Vespers are sung in monasteries, cathedrals and collegiate churches every day between 3 and 6 p.m. (See also **worship**.)

vestments

Ceremonial garments worn by priests and their assistants when performing a religious ritual. The wearing of vestments is an ancient practice, seen early on in the costume worn by the High Priest of Israel. They are rich in symbolism, extravagant in colour, and a powerful means of focusing attention. (See also **ephod**; **mitre**.)

vicarious atonement

A notion applied in Christian theology to Jesus's role as someone who suffered as a substitute for others. The Bible insists that Jesus's suffering was vicarious, in that he freely and out of love took the place of sinners, carrying their guilt, and enduring the punishment they were due. (See also **atonement**.)

vine

A frequently-used image in the Bible. For the Old Testament, the image of Israel as a vine is used by the poets and prophets to express the truth that she is a precious belonging of God's. God has high hopes for Israel, and his disappointment runs deep when she produces bitter fruits or is shrouded in barrenness. In the New Testament, Jesus himself is presented as the vine, from which the Church, as the branches, must draw its life force, if it is to prove fruitful. The image provides a key concept for Christian devotion, for it vividly makes the point that, apart from him, the Christian can achieve nothing that is effective or enduring. (See also **wine**.)

Virgin Birth

The doctrine that Jesus was born of a virgin mother through the actions of the Holy Spirit. The issue was not a priority for the early Church, and though it is spoken of in Matthew and Luke (both of these being later Gospels), there is little reference to it in the earliest writings. While stories of miraculous births were commonplace in the mythologies of the 1st century, the New Testament accounts of the Virgin Birth emerged from an understanding of what the gospel teaches. The theology of the early Church clearly required a human Jesus and a divine Son of God in one and the same person. The reality of Jesus's divinity was clearly declared by his resurrection; and the reality of his humanity needed comparable emphasis. Holding both these tenets of faith together required an action of God in the human situation to give the world the Christ. The Virgin Birth gives some answer to this theological need. (See also **Annunciation**; **miracle**; **Son of God**.)

Vishnu

An important Hindu God, the second in the Trimurti, understood to be the one who keeps the universe in being. He is thought of as the embodiment of mercy and goodness. Hindus believe he has come to earth on nine occasions – three manifestations in non-human form, one in hybrid form, and five in human form, the two most important of these being Rama and Krishna. (See also **Avatar**; **Juggernaut**; **Krishna**; **Trimurti**.)

vision

A special revelation of God's will enjoyed by individuals or, occasionally, a number of people. Sometimes visions are given in dreams, sometimes they are words heard in a particular encounter with God. A vision can also be a moment of understanding and clarity when the meaning of what is seen dawns by divine impulse. The visions of the later prophets of Israel are, by and large, elaborate and stylized, full of complex symbolism and arcane imagery. The most important visions in the New Testament are the reports of the appearances of the Risen Jesus. Other visions of the more prophetic type also appear in the New Testament, and revelatory dreams also feature. However, unlike other more speculative religions, the Old and New Testament revelations owe comparatively little to the experience of visions for the message they bring. (See also **revelation**.)

vocation

A divine summons for an individual to pursue a particular ministry, career, or task; also referred to as a *call* or *calling*. It is difficult to explain to those who have not experienced it how a growing sense of inner conviction, often reinforced by the ideas, counsel, and encouragement of others, can come to have a firm hold on a person. But there is no doubt that it happens, and many people – not just professional ministers or priests – hold a deep conviction that the career they are pursuing is more than simply a job, but is where God wants them to be.

voodoo

The popular religion of Haiti, also found in other parts of the West Indies and in parts of South America. It has come to be associated with powerful spirit forces of a sinister nature, and the fear they can induce. Originally a blend of Roman Catholicism and the nature religion of West Africa, voodooism allows its followers to attend church and voodoo temple with equal validity. In temple worship, a voodoo priest or priestess uses magical diagrams, songs, and prayer to call up the spirits of the voodoo world. These possess the worshippers, inducing a trance-like state, and also threatening those who are considered liable to punishment. Voodoo influence is a powerful force over the minds of its participants.

vows

Serious commitments undertaken to show loyalty to God, or to undertake some particular religious discipline. They are often heard in a situation of crisis, when an individual makes a bargain with God – promising certain actions, if God will retrieve the situation. Less self-interested promises are made out of a spirit of appreciation of God's goodness and love. (See also **oath**.)

Vulgate

An influential translation of the Old Testament into Latin, at the time of publication the universal language of communication. It was made by St Jerome in the 4th century AD. (See also **Old Testament**.)

W

Waldenses

A 12th-century reform movement within the Roman Catholic Church begun by a French merchant turned preacher, Peter Valdes or Waldo. Waldo refused to acknowledge the authority of the pope, veneration of the saints, and prayers for the dead. The Waldenses endured severe persecution, but a small community survived, and after the Reformation continued chiefly in Piedmont, Northern Italy.

washing

An important ritual of Jewish life and religion. Washing for health and hygiene purposes is prescribed in the Old Testament, while the clear symbolism of cleansing as a sign of purification emerges naturally from common practices. Priests and people both required ceremonial washing in preparation for worship, and by the time of the New Testament a complex system had been developed by the Pharisees for the particular purpose of ritual purification. Their obsession with externals, to the continual neglect of the inner needs, was challenged by Jesus, and became a source of his conflict with them. (See also **purification**.)

water

A notion which in the Bible develops a profound and almost sacred significance. In the Old Testament the presence of water is viewed with emotion as a sign of blessing, and rivers and wells are clearly acknowledged as signs of God's pleasure. Drought and desert are vivid illustrations of the reality of his wrath. The dramatic experience that leads Moses to find water in a rock, under the direction of God, is viewed by the nation as a crucial moment in her history. The great visions of the glorious Kingdom of God laid particular emphasis on the rivers of water that will flow deep and full through that wonderful place. At the same time, the Israelites had a deep fear of water, seeing it as a symbol of God's anger. The power of the sea was intimidating to a desert people. The story of the Flood haunted them, and the ordeal of the Red Sea crossing gave the Jews respect for the power of water and the dangers of the deep. The New Testament points up the symbolism of water, using it as a sign of the Holy Spirit: 'the living water that flows to eternal life' brings freshness and hope to the life of the believer. It is in this spirit that the use of water in baptism indicates the idea of renewal and life-giving power, as well as the symbolism of purification. (See also **baptism**; **purification**; **washing**.)

Westminster Confession of Faith

A credal statement drawn up as the main Presbyterian Confession of Faith in 1643. It retains a place of some significance in present-day Church life, as a required test of theological 'reliability' at the ordination of every minister and elder within the Presbyterian Church. It lays out the principal doctrines of the Christian faith from a Calvinist viewpoint, and has become the major confessional tool in Reformed Churches within the English-speaking world. (See also **Calvinism**; **Presbyteriansim**.)

wine

The fermented juice of the grape, associated with joy and celebration, and thus symbolically with the idea of spiritual gladness. While there are Biblical elements ranged clearly against the intoxicating effects of wine, there is also present in the Bible a recognition of the value of wine as part of a well-balanced lifestyle. With its significant role as a symbol of the blood of Christ in the central act of worship of the Church, it remains a potent metaphor within Christian thought. (See also **Eucharist**; **vine**.)

wisdom

A notion originally associated with the great teachings of the wise men of Israel, at first in oral form, and eventually written down in the *Wisdom Books* – Proverbs, Job, the Song of Songs, and Ecclesiastes, and (in the Apocryphya) Ecclesiasticus and the Wisdom of Solomon. Usually written in a highly-stylized form, the purpose of these writings was to give practical guidance about how to deal with the vagaries of life, all the time conveying a sense of religious dependence upon God. As Greek philosophy began to influence the wisdom literature of the Jews, the idea of wisdom itself began to be identified as an element of the divine being; and this identification may lie behind the New Testament concept of the *Logos*, or divine Word. The Bible certainly encourages respect for wisdom, seeing it as a worthy quality to attain, and since 'the fear of the Lord is the beginning of wisdom' there is no contradiction for someone pursuing wisdom while serving God. (See also **Bible**; **Job**; **proverbs**.)

witchcraft

The use of magical or psychic powers to control objects, events, or supernatural beings. Commonplace among Israel's pagan neighbours, witchcraft was roundly condemned by the religious leaders of Israel, being seen by them as a challenge to the authority of the one true God. In the New Testament the practice of witchcraft is also seen as a direct contradiction of God's power, the role of the Gospel being to liberate from its darkness anyone ensnared by its practices. (See also **occultism**.)

witness

Someone who saw something happen. The origins of the idea plainly lie in the realm of justice and evidence, but in theology the word has assumed overtones that are concerned with evangelistic endeavour – standing up for and speaking about the faith an individual believes in. The Greek word for 'martyr' means essentially someone who bears witness by death to faith in Christ. Witnessing has been understood by the church to be a major reason for its growth and continuing life. (See also **evangelical**.)

Word

A notion central to both Judaism and Christianity; also called the *Word of God*. It is God's Word that effects things in the world. God 'speaks', and this action brings things into existence, changes situations, or offers hope and deliverance. The whole of the work of the great prophets of Israel is to convey the Word of God that will challenge and save. Without this Word there is no religion or special relationship. Later, Greek philosophical influences began to infiltrate the theology of Judaism, notably the idea of *Logos*, the principle of rationality and wisdom. However, it was a particular Jewish conviction that to have the Word of God was in effect to have something of God's very self, to be in touch with his will in an intimate way. It is this sense which is conveyed by the New Testament notion that Jesus is the Word - the same

Word that in the beginning created the world and revealed God's will to Israel. (See also **truth**.)

works

A notion which summarizes a person's good deeds, righteous life, and correct religious observance. It became part of an important argument during the Reformation, which claimed to return to the New Testament principle that 'works' counted for nothing in the great reckonings of God. What really mattered was Christ's work at Calvary, and faith was to be in him, and not in good deeds. The interpretation of the Gospel as 'faith alone' is the crucial achievement of the reformers, who thought this to be the distinctive characteristic of the Christian faith. (See also **salvation**.)

World Council of Churches

An interdenominational gathering of churches from throughout the world, committed to seeking the unity of the Church. Founded in Amsterdam in 1948, it emerged from the ecumenical concerns of the 20th-century Church. It draws its membership from most of the main Christian denominations. The Roman Catholic Church until recently enjoyed only an 'observer' status, but this has now changed to a position of wholehearted involvement. With its headquarters in Geneva, it meets in Assembly every six or seven years, attended by representatives of all affiliated denominations. (See also **ecumenism**.)

worldly

A way of describing individuals bent on a life of totally secular living, without reference to God or personal spirituality. It is a code-word among those of an evangelical persuasion for the allurements, distractions, and attitudes of a society where God has been forgotten or excluded.

worship

Reverence offered to a divine being or supernatural power. Wherever gods are acknowledged, there follows an attitude of worship, and a format in which to express that worship – a religious ritual, by means of which people can declare their feelings of obligation or wonder. Clearly, the nature of the god will have a considerable influence upon the type of worship offered. If it is a terrifying and oppressive god, the worship of its frightened creatures will have a particular flavour and style. If it is a compassionate, holy, and glorious god, such as the God of Israel, then worship will reflect that understanding. The main ingredients of Israel's worship include a celebration of God's powerful nature as discovered in the form and wonder of the universe, an acknowledgement of human sin, and a consequent need to deal with God's holiness. This led to the sacrifices, sin offerings, and thanksgivings of Israel's religion. For Christianity, the reality of Jesus and his achievement of salvation was the main element in New Testament worship. The central act of worship was the Lord's Supper, which focused the emotions and thoughts of the early Church on the story of the Gospel and its meaning in their lives. (See also **holy**; **liturgy**; **Sabbath**; **shrine**; **synagogue**; **Vespers**.)

wrath of God

A notion which follows from the holy nature of God, who cannot abide sin, which is destructive to his purposes for the world. His response is like that of a king whose law has been flouted by disobedient subjects – anger, and a resolve to deal with the sin. The wrath of God is expressed in allowing the logic of sin to run its course, and the consequences of sinfulness to fall upon the heads of the perpetrators. The New Testament makes it clear that the full force of the law of God must be expressed if the integrity of creation and the nature of God are to be sustained. God cannot ignore sin's attack on him and on his creation. The Old Testament sacrificial system is seen as a partial response, deflecting God's anger away from the sinner to the sacrifice he brings. In the New Testament there is a more powerful response: the anger is directed at Jesus, 'the Lamb of God who takes away the sin of the world'. (See also **sacrifice**; **sin**.)

Y

Yahweh

The mysterious name by which the Hebrews knew God. It was never spoken in full, out of respect and awe, the consonants alone being used. The origins of the name are obscure, and there is debate as to quite how old it actually is, since according to the Book of Exodus the name was revealed to Moses for the first time. This is in conflict with the suggestion in Genesis 4.1 that the name was familiar in the earliest phases of Hebrew history. Whatever the origins, the name became distinctive for the living God worshipped by Israel, identifying the nation, and giving it a unique sense of its own character. They were, above all else, the people of Yahweh. (See also **God**; **Jehovah**.)

ying and yang

In the teaching of the Chinese religious leader, Lieh Tse, the positive and negative principles within creation. They are reflected in such opposites as night and day, dark and light, earth and heaven – ideas crucial to the world view of Taoism. (See also **Taoism**.)

yoga

The means by which, through a variety of specific exercises, control over the mind and body can be achieved. The aim is a concentration of the mind away from the transience of the world, in order to ponder the truly eternal and significant. In Hinduism, the physical serenity achieved through the discipline of the exercises is seen as a way of opening the life to Brahma, the goal of such meditations. This deeply religious function is in contrast with modern society's conception of yoga, which is often seen as nothing more than a way of keeping the body fit and supple. (See also **meditation**.)

yoni

See **lingam**

Z

Zadok

The chief priest of Judah, based in Jerusalem during the reigns of David and Solomon. He supported Solomon during civil unrest and was appointed High Priest. His descendants retained the position through many generations, at least until the second century BC. (See also **High Priest**.)

zealot

Anyone with a passionate devotion to a particular cause, and who desires to share that passion with others, whether they like it or not. Originally the Zealots were a particularly enthusiastic and dedicated group within Judaism, were devoted to the Law of God, and particularly resentful of any intrusion by the Roman authorities into the autonomy of Judaism. They were at the forefront of rebellion during the uprisings against Roman occupation in both AD 6 and AD 66. Jesus included at least one Zealot among his disciples, Simon the Zealot, and this may have confused his motives in the minds of some observers, who might have considered his goals to be political rather than spiritual.

Zen Buddhism

A form of Buddhism, dedicated to meditation, brought to Japan in the 12th century by monks returning from China. It had originated in India, then spread to China, where it adopted certain aspects of Taoism. The emphasis of Zen is for the individual to find personal enlightenment, encouraged by a simple life lived in harmony with nature, and sustained by forms of meditation which avoid complicated rituals and abstract thought. (See also **Buddhism**.)

Zion

One of the four hills on which Jerusalem is built. This association began to develop symbolic, suggestive overlays of meaning, which came to be synonymous with God's chosen dwelling-place and a focal point of his rule. In the imaginative symbolism of the

New Testament, the New Jerusalem of God's glorious future is considered to be 'Zion city', the heavenly dwelling-place of God and all his saints.

Zionism

The movement for a return of the Jewish people to their traditional homeland in Palestine, a desire which sustained Jews through all the turmoil of persecution, dispersion, and holocaust. Its modern expression began in the late 19th century with plans to colonize Palestine, and under the leadership of Theodore Herzl (1860–1904) it developed into a political programme designed to gain sovereign state rights over the territory. The establishment of the Jewish State in 1948 was seen as the realization of the Zionist dream. Zionism still operates as a political force, taking the form of a movement to encourage Jews throughout the world to return to Israel and to support its interests. (See also **dispersion**; **Judaism**.)

Zoroastrianism

A religion founded by the Iranian prophet Zoroaster (c. 630–c. 553 BC); also known as *Parsiism*. Now found mainly in India, it was thought to have influenced Judaism and Christianity in its development of a strong ethical viewpoint, and its belief in a bodily resurrection, eternal life, and a saviour who would come.